Essential Primary Grammar

Essential Primary Grammar

Debra Myhill

Susan Jones

Annabel Watson

Helen Lines

Open University Press

Open University Press
McGraw-Hill Education
McGraw-Hill House
Shoppenhangers Road
Maidenhead
Berkshire
England
SL6 2QL

email: enquiries@openup.co.uk
world wide web: www.openup.co.uk

and Two Penn Plaza, New York, NY 10121-2289, USA

First published 2016

A catalogue record of this book is available from the British Library

ISBN-13: 978-0-33-526238-0
ISBN-10: 0-33-526238-4
eISBN: 978-0-33-526239-7

Library of Congress Cataloging-in-Publication Data
CIP data applied for

Typeset by SPi-Global

Printed and bound by CPI Group (UK) Ltd, Croydon, CR0 4YY

Praise for this book

"This practical teacher, trainee guide to grammar is exactly what is needed today. In the current climate where grammar has an increased focus, there is a pressure for teachers to teach grammar to the test. This book gives an excellent research evidence based approach that puts the teaching of grammar firmly onto a book rich curriculum that not only enhances subject knowledge but also awakens an interest in the grammar."

Jo Tregenza, Senior Teaching Fellow and Head of Initial Teacher Training, University of Sussex, UK

"At last, the book we have been waiting for! Essential Primary Grammar perfectly combines clear, detailed subject knowledge, a rigorous research base and inspiring practical teaching ideas. The focus on using authentic texts throughout, exemplified with classic and easy to find titles will support teachers to be more adventurous, more creative and have more fun with their grammar teaching. Myhill et al manage to tackle some of the trickiest aspects of grammar with clarity and a lightness of touch that ensures the reader never feels they have been taken too far into the depths of linguistics. Every primary teacher needs a copy in their bag!"

*Rebecca Cosgrave, Primary English Adviser,
Babcock LDP*

"This is an important book that is grounded in research, proposing a convincing argument for the value of explicit grammar teaching and identifying important pedagogical principles. It is also extremely practical, explaining grammatical concepts in clear and helpful terms, and offering a range of engaging teaching activities for the classroom. The authors' enthusiasm and expertise mean that this is undoubtedly a 'must have' book for practitioners wanting to develop students' awareness of grammar and language topics more generally."

*Marcello Giovanelli, Assistant Professor in
English Education, University of Nottingham, UK*

Contents

List of contributors   *viii*
Acknowledgements   *ix*
Introduction   *x*

1 **A creative pedagogy for teaching grammar**   **1**

2 **The verb group**   **10**

3 **The noun group**   **22**

4 **The adverb group**   **36**

5 **Clauses**   **50**

6 **Sentences**   **65**

7 **Vocabulary**   **80**

8 **Standard English**   **87**

9 **The role of talk**   **101**

Endnote   *110*
References   *111*
Index   *112*

List of contributors

Debra Myhill, Susan Jones, Annabel Watson and **Helen Lines** are all former teachers, and now researchers at the Centre for Research in Writing at the University of Exeter. The Centre has researched many aspects of writing over a long period, including linguistic development in writing, the role of talk in the writing classroom, children's composing processes and their reflections on them, and the grammar–writing relationship. Currently, the team is following children in primary and secondary schools, mapping how their understanding of grammar and choices in writing develops over time, and working with Arvon to evaluate the impact that attending a residential 'Teachers as Writers' programme has on the teaching of writing.

Acknowledgements

This book owes a great debt to three linguists: David Crystal, Ronald Carter and Richard Hudson. We are not linguists and, in preparing this book, we have drawn heavily on the grammar and linguistic reference books produced by these academic linguists. More than this, we are grateful for their long-standing enthusiasm for grammar as a positive force in the curriculum, and for the generous support, often personal, that they have given us.

This book was written standing on the shoulders of giants!

Introduction

Grammar joke

Let's eat Grandma!

Let's eat, Grandma!

Punctuation SAVES LIVES!

There is a debate among linguists as to whether the word 'glamour' is derived from 'grammar'. You might think that there are few things that seem *less* related, but this harks back to the medieval sense of 'grammar' as specialised, esoteric and even occult knowledge — accessible to only a few studious individuals and epitomised in Merlin's collection of spells, *The Book of Gramarye*. While we can't promise you anything quite as exciting as a spell book, we would like to try to tap in to the idea that grammatical knowledge *can* be a little bit enchanting, unlocking language in a way that allows you to experiment, play and create.

In stark contrast to the medieval view, this book aims to make grammar accessible to all. It has two key purposes: to be a resource for developing knowledge of grammar, and to explain and exemplify a creative, contextualised approach to teaching it. This teaching approach is evidence based, founded on a body of research (e.g. Jones, Myhill & Bailey, 2013), which shows that children benefit from being taught in a way that uses examples from authentic texts, that makes connections between being a reader and being a writer, that explores the effects of words, phrases, sentences and paragraphs, and that encourages them to play with language in their own writing. This approach asks much of teachers: you have to know not only how to analyse texts grammatically, but also how to explain grammar to children, how to talk about effects in a way that is specific and contextualised, and how to help children to transfer knowledge of grammar into their own writing. Hence, in all of the chapters in this book that cover elements of grammar, we have included examples from real texts that could be used in primary classrooms, and ideas for teaching activities. We've also included some chapters that explain the pedagogy in more depth, in the hope that you will be able to use the principles to develop your own ideas and resources.

We believe that grammar is important, not because the curriculum and national tests require it to be taught, but because it is an important element of knowledge about language. Many teachers — even English specialists — have never been taught grammar explicitly, due to the fact that it largely fell out of favour in the 1970s and 1980s in light of evidence that old approaches to grammar had no impact on children's writing (e.g. Elley *et al.*, 1975). It's worth noting that these old pedagogies typically taught grammar as a separate lesson, focusing on definitions, exercises and labelling, without making links to the texts read and written during other lessons. It's easy for teachers who have only ever learned about grammar implicitly, and yet who consider themselves to be excellent readers and writers, to believe that it is an unnecessary and over-emphasised aspect of the curriculum.

Our own research paints a different picture. For many children, yes, exposure to language will be sufficient for them to pick up different linguistic structures and be able to use them in their writing. Some may even be able to use them effectively, with intent. However, extending that exposure with explicit teaching that involves open discussion, exploration, investigation and experimentation has a much *greater* impact on children's writing, as they begin to develop a wider repertoire of structures they can consider, select from and apply (Myhill *et al.*, 2012). Their deeper understanding of how language works enables them to exercise *conscious choice* in their writing, helping them to *craft* their work. While this may seem a tall order for KS1 in particular, the activities we've included demonstrate how even simple texts — like *Hairy Maclary* by Lynley Dodd or *Where the Wild Things Are* by Maurice Sendak, or even *Rosie's Walk* by Pat Hutchins — use particular patterns of language that can become models for children to play with.

This view of grammar is very different to one that is driven by accuracy or 'rules'. Our approach is not focused on eliminating errors or mistakes in children's use of language, nor on teaching them to speak or write 'correctly' or 'properly'. Indeed, children will often make more mistakes when they are trying out new, more sophisticated, grammatical patterns in their speech and writing, and they need to be encouraged to experiment, rather than stick only with what they know they can get right. Instead, we understand that grammar is an attempt to explain how words work together to create meaning: language evolves independently of the concepts and terminology we use to classify and describe it. Grammar is also an imperfect description of language: sometimes there are things that defy classification and areas where boundaries are blurred. You also need to be aware that there are multiple 'grammars': different versions of grammatical categories and terms. We're using the grammar of the current English National Curriculum here, but if you look for additional support online you may find yourself confronted by other types of terminology (e.g. gerunds!). The key is to build your knowledge slowly, look for resources that will help you to develop and consolidate your understanding of the concepts in this book, and keep applying these concepts to the real texts you encounter and teach.

The National Curriculum sets out, in the Grammar Annex, what primary children are expected to know in relation to grammar. It specifies what grammatical terms children are expected to know explicitly at the end of each year, and it also specifies what grammatical features they are expected to encounter during that year as part of their language experience. So, for example, in Year 2, children are expected to know the terms *noun* and *noun phrase*, and to be able to identify them. They are also expected to be introduced to subordination and co-ordination, but they do not need to know the terms *subordination* and *co-ordination*. This might involve an activity where you look at how conjunctions such as *when, because, and* or *but* are used in the books they are reading, or in their own writing. One thing is very clear, though: you need to know a lot more than your children do, and to develop confidence with grammar so that you can handle their questions and recognise their learning needs.

The first chapter of this book explains our pedagogical approach to embedding grammar within the teaching of writing. The chapters that follow it each focus on a particular grammatical strand: the first group focuses on grammatical elements at word and phrase level (the verb group, noun group and adverbial group), while the next looks at grammar at clause and sentence level. A vocabulary chapter looks at word families, and the links between spelling and grammar, and then a chapter on Standard English examines its distinctive features. The final chapter focuses on the importance of high-quality talk about language, drawing together the various strands of the book by showing how talk is the key to developing children's thinking about language.

The structure of this book is designed to develop your knowledge in a logical way, but it should also serve as a resource that can be dipped in to, to refresh or consolidate your understanding. We hope that you will find the explanations clear and the teaching ideas inspiring. Our hope is that all readers will find themselves at least a *little* beguiled by the idea that grammatical knowledge can become something that is empowering, playful and creative.

1

A creative pedagogy for teaching grammar

> **Grammar joke**
>
> Q: What's the difference between a cat and a comma?
> A: One has claws at the end of its paws and one is a pause at the end of a clause.

At the University of Exeter's Centre for Research in Writing, we have been investigating the contested issue of grammar teaching over many years. Based on our research findings, we believe that an effective pedagogy for writing *should* include grammar teaching that draws attention to the linguistic choices and possibilities available to children, and that has at its heart the creative shaping of text. This chapter explains this pedagogy and the reasons for it.

Grammar in the English National Curriculum

The view of grammar we are promoting is a *descriptive* one, which describes the grammar of language as it *is* used, rather than a *prescriptive* grammar, which sets out how grammar *should be* used. We are interested in developing learners' knowledge about how language works in different real-life contexts, and opening up for them the infinite repertoire of choices available to them as writers. This view is not a new one: the very first National Curriculum in England in 1989 had a clear focus on developing children's knowledge about language — or grammar — through exploration of different text types, and that emphasis is still clear today. Knowledge about language means making what is implicitly understood explicit, and having a language to talk about grammar helps in this process. Remind yourself how the current statutory requirement refers to these concepts.

> The grammar of our first language is learnt naturally and implicitly through interactions with other speakers and from reading. Explicit knowledge of grammar is, however, very important as it gives us more conscious control and choice in our language. Building this knowledge is best achieved through a focus on grammar within the teaching of reading, writing and speaking.
>
> . . . The grammatical terms that pupils should learn are labelled as 'terminology for pupils'. They should learn to recognise and use the terminology through discussion and practice.
>
> (Foreword to English Appendix 2: Vocabulary, grammar and punctuation)

- Is there anything here that you personally disagree with?
- In your own classroom, how helpful have you found it to have a shared language — a metalanguage — to enable you to talk with children about their reading and writing?

A *prescriptive* view of grammar lays out rules about what is considered 'correct' and 'incorrect' use of language, often illustrated through specially constructed examples — you may well have learned some of these rules for 'proper English' when you were at school, such as 'Never split an infinitive' or 'Don't end a sentence with a preposition' and — depending on your age — you may have practised labelling 'parts of speech' in decontextualised exercises and drills. A prescriptive view of grammar is strongly associated with the avoidance or correction of error in children's writing, especially non-Standard English usage such as 'we was' instead of 'we were' or 'gotten' instead of 'got'. Viewed from this perspective, and especially in the popular press, grammar is seen as an antidote to 'falling standards' in education, a return to the 'rigour' of traditional values and teaching methods, or 'back to basics' as the most recent curriculum changes were reported.

- These different views of grammar are often presented as opposites, in conflict with one another. Do you think this matters? Is there any tension for *you* in the way you view grammar?

Of course, what *is* new in the current National Curriculum is the statutory testing of children's grammatical knowledge at ages 7 and 11. Remind yourself of some typical Key Stage 2 test items:

---

2 Tick one box in each row to show which word completes the sentence correctly.

Sentence	good	well
He plays the drums_____.		
The concert was _____.		
I had a _____ idea.		
The children worked _____ as a team.		

19 Place three full stops and three capital letters in the correct places in the text below.

it was hot and dry richard could feel the sun on his back he took a long drink of water

(Grammar, punctuation and spelling Paper 1, DfE, 2014)

- What aspects of children's knowledge about language are tested here?
- What might children's test results tell you about their writing ability?

Key teaching principles

The research carried out at the University of Exeter is underpinned by a view of the importance of teaching grammar *in the context of children's writing*, not as a body of separate knowledge learned for its own sake. Contextualised grammar teaching is explicit about how language works, and about how language choices construct meanings in different contexts, using the correct grammatical terminology as part of that explicitness. But the teaching focus is on the writing being undertaken rather than on a grammar feature or terminology itself. Teaching approaches centre on exploration of language use in real texts, rather than transmission of facts about grammar or artificial exercises. It means putting teaching about writing first. This might sound very obvious, but in our research we have seen how easy it is for teachers to get drawn into 'ticking off' grammatical features from the statutory requirement of the National Curriculum by introducing and practising them through decontextualised examples. This is completely understandable given the pressures of national testing and teachers' accountability for test results, but these pressures make it doubly important that classroom practice is grounded in principles that promote meaningful connections between grammar and writing. Our key teaching principles are:

Always link a grammar feature to its effect on the writing.

Use grammatical terms, but explain them through examples.

Encourage high-quality discussion about language and effects.

Use authentic examples from authentic texts.

Use model patterns for children to imitate.

Support children to design their writing by making deliberate language choices.

Encourage language play, experimentation and risk-taking.

The specific theoretical thinking informing each of the principles, and examples of how each one could be realised in practice, are shown in more detail below.

Making connections

Always link a grammar feature to its effect on the writing

The goal of contextualised grammar teaching is to support children's writing development, not to learn grammar. This means being explicit with children about the learning purpose. So, for example, rather than saying 'Today we are learning what a prepositional phrase is', you might say, 'Today we are learning how to describe the setting for our story by using prepositional phrases.' Tying a grammatical feature to its effect on meaning in a specific context is part of beginning to understand the writer's craft and the possibilities open to a writer. The emphasis on context also helps avoid redundant learning, such as 'complex sentences are good sentences' or 'add adjectives to make your writing more descriptive'. Children have learned various incorrect 'rules' about writing caused by imprecision and poor connections being made between a grammar point and how it shapes meaning in the text being considered, so it is important for you to ask, whenever a grammatical term is being used in a lesson, 'Why am I discussing this here? What do I want them to learn about writing as a consequence?'

A classroom example

Context: Writing fairy tales

Learning focus: How fairy tales use short, simple noun phrases to describe characters, settings and objects

Connections between grammar and writing: Through discussion and close reading/close listening to fairy tales, the teacher draws out that many fairy tales use short, premodified noun phrases, often drawing on a restricted stock of vocabulary that recurs in many tales — e.g. *a wicked stepmother; a beautiful princess; a handsome prince; the enchanted forest; a golden apple* . . .

Using grammar terminology

Use grammatical terms, but explain them through examples

Using appropriate metalanguage to discuss language can help teachers and children to be precise; it allows for more succinct talk about reading and writing. However, there is always a danger that the terminology obscures the learning focus of the lesson, or indeed *becomes* the learning focus ('Who can tell me what a verb is?'). At its worst, terminology can become a barrier to learning, and we have certainly observed children struggling to remember what terms mean, confusing one term with another, or becoming anxious when trying to cope with the level of abstraction that providing definitions of terms requires of them. In any case, simply being able to identify and define grammatical labels is not related to writing skills: there are children who can 'talk the talk' but do not understand the terms they use; just as there are children who ably use grammatical constructions in their writing but cannot label the features they have used.

Teachers' attempts to simplify metalanguage can leave children confused — for example, by viewing 'a drop-in clause' as anything that appears in a sentence with parenthetical commas — and of course this could apply to a single word, a phrase or a clause. Research has shown that children at an early age are able to cope with the use of formal grammatical metalanguage and the concepts it refers to when terminology is used regularly and purposefully in specific contexts, alongside examples and patterns of the language feature under study. Seeing and hearing examples makes the learning more concrete and allows children to access and play with a particular structure, and discuss its effect, even if they do not remember the grammatical name. Children may well need to explore the grammatical concept first — for example, by manipulating relative clauses in sentences — before moving on to labelling. In the classroom example below, the term 'modal verb' is used, but the support of a resource simply listing the modal verbs, and the activity of speculating about a character's actions, enables children to access the writing task, even if their grammatical understanding of modal verbs is limited.

A classroom example

Context: Writing advice to a character facing a dilemma at a key point in a story

Learning focus: How different levels of possibility can be expressed through modal verbs

Activity: Provide modal verbs on cards: *can; could; may; might; must; shall; should; will; would; ought to.*

In a discussion of *The Balaclava Story* by George Layton, children use the modal verbs to speculate as to what George will do when he finds Norbert's balaclava, and the possible consequences.

They use some of the modal verbs to write a letter of advice explaining what they think George *should/might/must* do.

The importance of talk

Encourage high-quality discussion about language and effects

The teaching materials used in our research projects have always included multiple opportunities for classroom talk about language choices and their effects. One danger of teaching grammar in the context of writing, particularly when teachers feel under pressure of time or assessment outcomes, is that teaching becomes overly didactic and children learn 'formulas' for writing, such as 'use a variety of sentence types', rather than understanding their impact on the text. Teacher explanations of grammar are important in initiating learning, but linguistic understanding, like all learning, cannot simply be transmitted directly from teacher to child. Talk is a critically important tool in securing meaningful learning about language. Indeed, it is so important that the final chapter of this book is dedicated entirely to talking about writing!

Exploratory talk that invites discussions about the grammar feature being studied, and that explores choices and possibilities, will help children make meaningful connections between grammar and writing and encourage them to take ownership of decision-making in writing. Active discussion about language and effects may be the key to moving children from superficial or rote learning about language (for example, 'use adjectives for description') to deep learning (for example, seeing that some adjectives are redundant because the noun itself is descriptive). We have found from our research that teachers who are confident in their grammatical subject knowledge are more likely to open up and push forward classroom discussions about language choices, rather than closing them down just as they are getting interesting! They are also more likely to probe children's understanding through well-chosen questions, supported with clear explanations and examples, and to develop with children a vocabulary for discussing the effectiveness of their writing.

A classroom example

Context: Writing fictional narrative

Learning focus: How the use of short sentences can create pace and tension in narrative

Activity: In pairs, children read the extract from *Skellig* by David Almond where Mina and Michael look for Skellig in the abandoned house. They find the six shortest sentences then discuss why the writer might have chosen to use so many short sentences. What part do they play in the narrative structure of this incident? How well do they work for the reader?

Using real texts

Use authentic examples from authentic texts

If you are old enough to remember labelling parts of speech or parsing sentences when you were at school, it's highly likely that the examples you practised on did not come from real texts, but were artificially generated to exemplify a grammar point. If you also learned to read with Janet and John books, you would have had a double dose of artificially constructed sentences! It *can* sometimes be useful to construct sentences that show or practise the use of a particular feature — and, of course, it can be very powerful to use your own texts to model a particular type of writing — but the principle of using authentic examples from authentic texts to exemplify grammar points, whenever possible, is designed to strengthen the links between reading and writing. Young writers need to explore what real writers do and the choices they make. Using authentic texts does more than avoid the pitfalls of grammar examples that have no resonance of truth (*I see two kittens. Look, John. See the two kittens.*). It links the community of school writers to the broader community of writers, and allows teachers to choose texts that will motivate their children. There will be many opportunities for using the texts you are teaching for reading to develop understanding of the grammar of the author's craft and how writing has been played with to achieve rhetorical goals.

A classroom example

Context: Writing poetry

Learning focus: How vivid description is created through verb choices

Activity: Listen to a recording of Ted Hughes reading his poem 'Wind' and share initial ideas about the most powerful words used to describe the storm.

Highlight the verbs on a copy of the poem. Individually or in pairs, children steal the ones they like best and use them in any sequence and any combination with other words in the poem to write a new poem describing a powerful wind. They compare their poem with the original and answer the question: Which do you like best and why?

The power of imitation

Use model patterns for children to imitate

Imitation is often thought of in negative terms, as unoriginal low-level copying, or even a form of cheating. But learning by imitating models (mimesis) has a very long history as a powerful tool to support initial learning about a text. Imitation is not the same as copying — it involves some kind of re-creation of grammatical patterns or ideas, rather than a direct duplication, and is best thought of as a scaffold that allows children to try out new structures and play with new forms of expression. While the precise grammatical metalanguage may be used to describe the pattern, imitation allows the young writer to practise and manipulate the structure without necessarily being able to label it grammatically, helping to embed new structures cognitively within the student's writing repertoire, and fostering success. Creative imitation is the first step in creating original combinations.

A classroom example

Context: Writing to persuade

Learning focus: How an effective opening to an emotive campaign text can be achieved using one-word sentences followed by a rhetorical question

Model text for imitation:

Beaten. Neglected. Starved. Will you help feed a dog like Archie until we can find him a home?

When we found Archie, he weighed 3.2kg — just half what he should have. Thankfully, he was brought to one of our rescue centres . . .

(RSPCA advertisement)

Making design choices

Support children to design their writing by making deliberate language choices

Writing is a complex act of decision-making, encompassing choices about content, structure and layout, sentence lengths and types, and vocabulary. The phrase 'conscious control' draws on the principle of giving more autonomy to the writer and less to the teacher, of making choices more visible in order to open up the writing process and encourage children to take responsibility for shaping and controlling their own texts — 'designing writing' rather than just 'doing writing'. Seeing writing as a design process highlights the need to plan a text that will fulfil a specific purpose for a specific audience, and embodies the notion of language as putty that can be shaped and crafted in an infinite variety of ways. In the classroom example below, the choice of 'best ending' is a genuinely open one; an activity like this encourages children to consider possible alternatives and to understand that writing is a process of making choices.

Playful experimentation

Encourage language play, experimentation and risk-taking

The final pedagogic principle is important because unless young writers enjoy what they are doing, are engaged with their learning and *want* to write, then the other principles will stay stuck as theory rather than practical reality. Writing is fun, and playfulness and experimentation help writers to see the elasticity of language, the possibilities it affords.

A classroom example

Context: Writing a speech

Learning focus: How sentence length and sentence structure can be used for rhetorical effect in the closing paragraph of a persuasive speech

Activity: In pairs, children are given sentences from the final paragraph of a persuasive speech, each sentence on a separate strip of paper. They are given two sets of the same sentences and create two versions of the ending of the speech. They choose their preferred version and explain their choice.

We want young writers to push language to its limits and test out its possibilities, and this is a principle that applies to children of all abilities. Able writers often play safe and avoid trying new ways of writing; weaker writers are often dogged by fear of failure; yet all professional writers understand that not all ideas work the first time round and coming up with things that don't quite work is part of the creative process. Of course, the notion of playfulness runs directly counter to a prescriptive view of grammar that emphasises rules, accuracy and the remediation of error, and highlights that writing is about pushing boundaries and trying out different ways of expressing thoughts and ideas.

A classroom example

Context: Writing poetry

Learning focus: How imaginative and important ideas can be described through noun phrases

Activity: Collapse Kit Wright's poem *The Magic Box* using Collapser.* This will create a list of all the words in the poem in alphabetical order without any punctuation. Invite children to use only the words in the list to create noun-phrase descriptions of special things or experiences that they would want to save for ever in a magic box. After they have created a few, model with them some very imaginative, playful things to go in the box, and encourage them to find more possibilities in the collapsed text.

This playful activity leads well into a shared reading of the poem and discussion of Kit Wright's special things. The poem can then be used as a model text for children to re-create their own personalised version of the poem.

*Collapser is a piece of free software that will collapse poems for you; it can be found at: www.englishandict.co.uk/resources/wordlab/collapser.html

The pedagogical approaches outlined in this chapter encourage teachers to teach writing in a manner that gives children explicit guidance about how to write and actively develops their metalinguistic knowledge, but this is overlaid with playful activities that allow exploration and experimentation with new knowledge. There is a danger sometimes that explicit teaching becomes formulaic, with children learning that being a 'good' writer is about putting certain things into your writing, like lots of adjectives before a noun, or connectives, or 'powerful' verbs rather than 'ordinary' verbs. The risk with this kind of learning is that there is no discussion of the effectiveness of a string of adjectives, or whether ideas are well linked by connectives, or whether an ordinary verb might be just the right choice. Young writers need help learning how to communicate through writing, how to express themselves and their ideas, and how to help their readers understand what they are trying to say. Author and poet John Dougherty, chair of the Society of Authors, Children's Writers and Illustrators Group, has criticised how writing is taught, arguing that:

> We're teaching them it means stuffing writing with adjectives, rather than that good writing is about communication, and will vary depending on what you're trying to communicate, what kinds of emotions you're trying to stir up, what kind of character you're trying to put into their minds. (Flood, 2015)

Our pedagogical approach puts the emphasis on what language can do, rather than on what writers should do, or must not do. It is strongly supportive in enabling children to make independent choices in their own writing through recognising what other writers do, and thus helps to give them greater ownership of their writing. We firmly believe that this equips children to be confident and effective writers in school, out of school and beyond schooling — young writers who become lifelong writers.

2

The verb group

What you need to know

The verb is the powerhouse of a sentence, or a clause. Many people will quickly tell you that every sentence must have a verb (not true, but we'll come to that later) and in many ways the verb is the engine of the sentence, driving its meaning. Yet the verb is a complex word class and is often poorly understood in all its breadth. In this chapter, we will focus on developing broad understanding of the verb. Much of this grammatical knowledge is for you as a teacher as it will help you handle children's misunderstandings about verbs. It will also help you understand clauses and sentence structure, which we will be looking at in later chapters. The way that sentences are structured and built up from phrases and clauses is known as syntax, and we are aware from our research that syntax is an area that many teachers are less confident with, and that having a secure understanding of verbs is the key to understanding clauses.

Understanding verbs and verb phrases

The verbs be *and* have

Perhaps it will surprise you to know that the most commonly occurring verbs in written text are the verbs *be* and *have*, yet many people don't really notice them as verbs. Have a look at your local newspaper, or a children's book, or your bedside novel, and you will find many, many examples of variations on the verbs *be* and *have*. These verbs are important because they link pieces of information and show relationships, and they tell us that certain things exist. Look at the extract below from E.B. White's *Charlotte's Web*, when Fern first meets Wilbur, the pig. The verb *were* links together the information that Fern's eyes are red from crying; and the verb *was* tells us that the scratching noise exists.

> Fern came slowly down the stairs. Her eyes <u>were</u> red from crying. As she approached her chair, the carton wobbled, and there <u>was</u> a scratching noise.

It is very helpful for children to understand that *be* and *have* are verbs, and to recognise all the various forms of these verbs. The diagram below shows all the possible variations of *be* and *have*; helpfully, these verbs are *always* verbs, whereas with many other words in a sentence, we have to work out whether it is a verb, or a noun, or an adjective, depending on its context.

<blockquote>
am is are were was

been being be
</blockquote>

<blockquote>
have has had

having
</blockquote>

Lexical verbs

Lexical verbs are the verbs that teachers are usually referring to when they say a verb is a 'doing' word   they are the verbs that carry a meaning. If we need to look up the meaning of a verb in a dictionary, it is likely to be a lexical verb. However, because the 'doingness' of lexical verbs is not always obvious, it is helpful to think about lexical verbs in three groups: action verbs, reporting verbs and sensing verbs. It's not at all important for children to be able to categorise verbs in this way, but it does help classroom conversations about verbs and enables children to understand that verbs without any obvious action are, nonetheless, verbs. Some examples from each group are given below.

Action verbs: these verbs express an action, such as *jump, dance, eat* or *ache*. They do also express actions that are less obviously active, such as *organise, lead* or *survive*.

Reporting verbs: these verbs tend to relate to speech and how something is said, such as *whisper, suggest, exclaim* or *shout*.

Sensing verbs: these verbs express thinking, feeling or understanding, and include verbs such as *believe, know, imagine, enjoy, fear, see* or *hear*.

Commands are always lexical verbs. Have a look at a recipe in a cookery book and notice how the instructions are lexical verbs (e.g. *cut, slice, stir, boil, simmer*). Exciting moments in a narrative plot often have a lot of lexical verbs; have a look at another extract from *Charlotte's Web*, just after Fern has opened the carton with Wilbur, the pig, in it:

> She <u>closed</u> the carton carefully. First she <u>kissed</u> her father, then she <u>kissed</u> her mother. Then she <u>opened</u> the lid again, <u>lifted</u> the pig out, and <u>held</u> it against her cheek.

Auxiliary verbs and verb phrases

Auxiliary verbs are sometimes called 'helper' verbs because in English they help us to form verb phrases that can express subtle differences in meaning, often related to time, tense or mood (active or passive). One of the reasons the verbs *be* and *have* are so commonly occurring in English is because they can be used as verbs in their own right (as in the first *Charlotte's Web* example, above) or as auxiliary verbs. The auxiliary verbs go before a lexical verb to create a verb phrase. If we take the first sentence from the second *Charlotte's Web* extract, we can change it from a **simple verb phrase** with just one lexical verb (*closed*) to more **complex verb phrases** with one or two auxiliary verbs before the lexical verb. Each new version of the original simple verb phrase gives subtly different information about Fern closing the carton:

> She closed the carton carefully.
>
> She is closing the carton carefully.
>
> She was closing the carton carefully.
>
> She had closed the carton carefully.
>
> She had been closing the carton carefully.

We also use *do* as an auxiliary verb, especially to form questions:

> Did she close the carton carefully?
>
> Do you want dinner now or later?
>
> Does she know that I can't come?

A sub-group of auxiliary verbs is the **modal verb** group. These are verbs that express possibility, certainty or tentativeness, and they are a small group of very common verbs:

> shall should can could
> might may must will would

Modal verbs also help to form verb phrases and allow us to express different degrees of possibility or assertiveness. Look here at how the original simple verb phrase telling us about Fern closing the carton can be expressed differently with modal verbs forming complex verb phrases:

> She closed the carton carefully.
>
> She should have closed the carton carefully.
>
> She might have been closing the carton carefully.
>
> She must close the carton carefully.

If you are confident in understanding the difference between lexical verbs and auxiliary verbs, and between simple verb phrases and complex verb phrases, you have a really strong foundation for understanding other aspects of verbs and syntax. Indeed, in the classroom, helping children understand that all the variations of *be* and *have* are verbs, and helping them understand the idea of a verb phrase, which might be one verb or a sequence of verbs, is really giving them building-block understanding of verbs that will support learning about sentences and clauses.

Why not test out your new knowledge by reading the extract below from Roald Dahl's *Matilda* and seeing if you can find the verb phrases and determine which are lexical verbs, and which are auxiliary verbs, including which are modal verbs. (Answers at the end of the chapter.)

> The nice thing about Matilda was that if you had met her casually and talked to her you would have thought she was a perfectly normal five-and-a-half-year-old child. She displayed almost no outward signs of her brilliance and she never showed off. 'This is a very sensible and quiet little girl' you would have said to yourself. And unless for some reason you had started a discussion with her about literature or mathematics, you would never have known the extent of her brain-power.

Understanding tense and aspect

Past and present tense

If you have studied a modern foreign language, or if you did Latin at school, you may know the names of lots of different tenses — for example, pluperfect, future or conditional — but did you know that different languages have differing numbers of tenses? In English, there are only two tenses — the present and the past. They express simply whether something is happening now, in the present, or whether it has already happened, in the past. Grammatically, a tense involves **inflection**, a change to the spelling of a word, to indicate the time change:

I walk	I walked
You think	You thought
She looks	She looked
They run	They ran

In English, regular verbs form the past tense by adding -ed to the base form, or infinitive form, of the verb, as you can see with *walk* and *look* in the examples above. But English, being a language rich with irregularities, also has many irregular verbs that form the past tense differently, as here with *think* and *run*. When toddlers are learning to talk, they will often create a regular past tense ending on an irregular verb — *I runned to Mummy* — which shows just how clever they are at picking up the principles of grammar in English, even if it does sometimes let them down! Most native speakers have very few problems with the English irregular verbs, but children learning English as an Additional Language (EAL) will often need explicit help learning these irregular forms.

When we write, the way we manage tense is important in crafting meaning. In narratives, we can choose whether we are going to tell the story in the present tense or in the past tense. Many narratives are told in the past tense — think of fairy tales beginning 'Once upon a time' or 'Long, long ago', signalling the past tense. Julia Donaldson's *The Gruffalo* is written in the past tense — 'A mouse took a walk through the deep dark wood' — as is J.K. Rowling's *Harry Potter and the Philosopher's Stone* — 'Mr and Mrs Dursley, of number four, Privet Drive, were proud to say that they were perfectly normal, thank you very much.' The past tense makes the narrative feel like a re-telling of a story, one that has already happened.

But a story told in the present tense is unfolding before your eyes and the reader is sharing in the immediacy of a story happening in real time. Anna Kemp's young children's story *Dogs don't do Ballet*, Janet and Allan Ahlberg's *Burglar Bill*, and Michael Rosen's *We're Going on a Bear Hunt* are all told in the present tense. Although Key Stage 1 children are unlikely to write a story themselves in the present tense, you can help them talk about the difference between a story told in the past and one told in the present. With confident Key Stage 2 writers, you might encourage them to experiment with writing a story in the present tense and discussing how the writer is inviting the reader to share in the experience as the story unfolds.

We also use the present tense in information and explanation texts, where the use of present tense suggests that a fact is universally true or timeless. Karen Wallace's beautiful dual narrative about the life cycle of an eel exemplifies this. For example, she explains that 'Eels arrive in Europe around Christmas time. They wait offshore until spring, and as they wait they turn into elvers.' Being able to recognise the past and present tense will help children to make appropriate choices in their own writing, and will help you discuss with them if they have not sustained a tense choice across the whole piece of writing.

You will notice that the present and past tense are always simple verb phrases, composed of just one lexical verb. This is because it is the inflection that does the job of telling us whether it is past or present. But, as you already know, we can form many variations of complex verb phrases with auxiliaries and lexical verbs. These complex verb phrases express many of the more subtle aspects of time. We often indicate that an event will happen in the future by using the auxiliary *will*:

We will eat in the morning.

You will apply to university when you are older.

But we do also communicate that things will happen in the future using a range of other auxiliary constructions and adverbs:

You <u>are leaving</u> tomorrow.

You <u>go</u> to France on Tuesday.

What <u>am I doing</u> later today?

Finite and non-finite verbs

A **finite verb** is one that inflects to show tense and person; it is called finite because it is finished or complete. It usually tells you who is doing the action of the verb. A **non-finite** verb does not show tense, and does not tell you who is 'doing' the verb, although you may well be able to guess from the context of the rest of the sentence. There are three forms of non-finite verb, as follows.

The present participle (the -ing form): *I was <u>walking</u>; they were <u>dancing</u>*

The past participle (usually an -ed form): *You had <u>walked</u>; they had <u>danced</u>*

The infinitive: *(to) <u>walk</u>; (to) <u>dance</u>*

While the present participle is always the -ing form of the verb, there are many irregular past participles that are not -ed forms, so you need to be alert to these (for example, *they had <u>sung</u>; you have <u>gone</u>*).

When you have a complex verb phrase, it is very easy to distinguish finite verbs from non-finite verbs, as the finite verb is always first, or on its own, in the verb phrase, and all the verbs that follow are non-finite. So if you look again at the complex verb phrases we discussed earlier, you can see that the finite verb (in bold) is first, followed by the non-finite verbs:

She **closed** the carton carefully.

She **is** closing the carton carefully.

She **was** closing the carton carefully.

She **had** closed the carton carefully.

She **had** been closing the carton carefully.

She **should** have closed the carton carefully.

You can see that the finite verb inflects for tense, because if you rewrite each of these examples in a different tense, it is only the finite verb that changes, and all the non-finite verbs remain the same. The exception here is the modal verb, *should*, which stays the same: modal verbs are always finite.

She **closes** the carton carefully.

She **was** closing the carton carefully.

She **is** closing the carton carefully.

She **has** closed the carton carefully.

She **has** been closing the carton carefully.

She **should** have closed the carton carefully.

Aspect: progressive and perfect(ive)

Aspect is the grammatical term that refers to how verb phrases can tell us more about when an event happened. Tense can tell us only that something is happening now in the present, or in the past, but aspect can give us more subtle information about the time frame of actions, particularly whether the action is completed or whether it is still continuing. The National Curriculum draws attention to the **progressive** aspect and the **perfect** aspect. These are useful constructions because they help us to convey whether an action is completed or whether it is still continuing.

- The progressive generally describes events that are in progress rather than completed. It is formed using the present participle of the verb, preceded by the past or present tense of 'have'.
- The perfect generally describes events that have been completed. The perfect is formed using the past participle of the verb, preceded by the present or past tense of the verb 'have'.

Have a look at the examples in the box below, and consider the different things they communicate about dancing.

Present progressive:	*I am dancing in my bedroom.*
Past progressive:	*I was dancing in my bedroom.*
Present perfect:	*She has danced for many years.*
Past perfect:	*She had danced for many years.*

Each version expresses something subtly different.

- The present progressive tells us the dancing is happening now and is still in progress.
- The past progressive tells us that the dancing happened in the past, but describes a time when it was still in progress.
- The present perfect tells us the dancer still dances and has done so over time.
- The past perfect tells us the dancer no longer dances but that s/he did dance in the past.

These different aspects allows us to communicate subtly different information about an activity. There is a difference between saying 'I danced in my bedroom then fell asleep', which is a sequence of events, and 'I was dancing in my bedroom when I remembered my homework', which tells us that remembering the homework happened while the dancing was still continuing. It can also help writers to communicate layers of time, such as a past-tense reference to something that happened further in the past: 'I was dancing in the competition because my father had taught me that winning was important.' Sometimes children, especially EAL children, need help understanding these subtle differences, especially when narrating events in a story or a report.

Understanding the active and passive voice

The **active voice** and the **passive voice** allow writers to make different choices about where the information in a clause is placed, and what information to reveal. The active voice is normally the most clear and direct. In the examples below, the first example of the passive withholds from us the information that it was the Chancellor that raised income tax, and in the second version we have to wait until the end of the sentence to find out that it was the Chancellor.

Active voice: The Chancellor raised income tax.

Passive voice: Income tax was raised.

Passive voice: Income tax was raised by the Chancellor.

So a sentence is in the active voice when the **subject** of the sentence performs the action in the sentence; here it is the Chancellor who does the raising of the income tax.

A sentence is in the passive voice when the subject of the sentence has the action in the sentence done to it by someone else. So, in the passive example above, the subject — 'income tax' — is raised by the Chancellor.

The passive voice is created using the auxiliary 'be' verb, plus the past participle — another example of the versatility of auxiliary verbs in English!

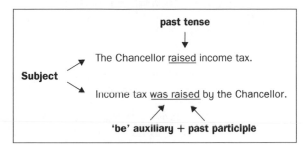

Using the active voice is often recommended as a clearer, more direct way of writing, and overuse of the passive is not wise. However, there are times when the passive voice is a very useful choice because it can help you.

- withhold information about who did the action — 'The window was broken'; 'Hospital spending has been cut'
- create an objective, detached voice; this is often used in science writing to focus on the science activity rather than the scientist conducting it — 'The test tubes were filled with magnesium' rather than 'We put magnesium in the test tubes'
- foreground the action rather than the doer of the action — 'The injured horse was put down by the duty vet'; in narrative, this is useful for creating different emphases
- maintain the cohesion across two sentences — 'The children stared with surprise at the strange giant. The giant was distressed by all the eyes upon him' rather than 'The children stared with surprise at the strange giant. Their eyes on him distressed the giant.'

Teaching activities

Language detectives: Investigating the curious case of the verb phrase

Learning objective: To develop grammatical understanding of how modal, auxiliary and lexical verbs are ordered in a verb phrase

Arrange children to work in groups of four. Invent a name for your detectives, such as the St Mary's Language Detective Agency, and create envelope address labels for this agency. Select ten sentences from a book or a text you are reading together, and reproduce these ten sentences, each on a strip of paper. Put these strips into an envelope for each group, with the detective agency name label on it. You might like to decorate these envelopes with other symbols of being a detective, such as spyglasses, tweezers, gloves, etc.

Display on a whiteboard or poster the three different verb groups (see boxes below: the modal verbs; the auxiliary verbs; and a sample of lexical verbs). Recap on the children's understanding of these. Ask children to underline all the verb phrases in each of the sentences, and then to see if they can work out the order in which these types of verb occur in a verb phrase. Then come together as a whole class to discuss the findings of the detectives and to see if they have found a solution. Using a whiteboard with modals, auxiliaries and lexical verbs colour-coded may act as a visual support here.

MODAL VERBS	AUXILIARY VERBS	SOME LEXICAL VERBS
can could will would	am is are was were	jump think eat play twist
might may must shall	been being have has	wait reply talk investigate
should	had having	explore

Talk about it!

This activity creates two different opportunities for talk: the group talk exploring complex verb phrases and their order, and the whole-class talk discussing the results. The group talk will be very exploratory, whereas the whole-class talk should secure the understanding.

- During the group talk, ask the group questions to establish their understanding of modal, lexical and auxiliary verbs. These might include questions such as:
  - » Which one is a modal verb?
  - » How do you know that is an auxiliary verb?
  - » Can you give me examples of any other lexical verbs?
- During the whole-class feedback, draw out their understanding of the order of modals, auxiliaries and lexical verbs in a verb phrase. You might include questions such as:
  - » What patterns have you noticed here?
  - » Can you think of an example where the lexical verb is not last? (There isn't one!)

Notes for teachers

1. For younger children, or to differentiate, use sentences with only one verb phrase per sentence, and choose sentences where the lexical verb is very obviously active.

2.   Remember that *be* and *have* verbs are auxiliaries only when they are followed by a lexical verb (as in *I am waiting for you; He has eaten his dinner*). If *be* and *have* are the only verb, they are not auxiliaries but lexical verbs in their own right (as in *I am a doctor; He has several new teeth*).

3.   The answer to the investigation is that verb phrases are always formed in the order: MODAL + AUXILIARY + LEXICAL.

Then and now: Exploring past and present tense in diaries

Learning objective: To understand how diary writing uses the present tense for diary comment and the past tense to narrate things that have happened

In advance, choose a book written for children in diary format, such as those listed a little below. Ideally, this book will be shared with the class as a text to enjoy, and the focus on tense woven in to work on the book. Choose several short extracts from the book where some are written in the past and some in the present tense. Create two spaces in the room — one for THEN and one for NOW — and ask the class to stand up. Read each extract aloud and ask them to decide if what is being written about happened in the past or now, and to reflect that decision by going to the space designated THEN or NOW.

Follow up this activity by looking at the diary extracts together as a class, preferably using a whiteboard where you can colour the past and present tense examples in different colours. Draw out their understanding of how the diary both records events and things that have happened, and the diary writer's private thoughts, comments and reflections on those events.

Some examples of diary texts suitable for primary

*   *Diary of a Killer Cat* by Anne Fine (particularly suitable for younger children)
*   *Dandelion Clocks* by Rebecca Westcott
*   *Diary of a Wimpy Kid* by Jeff Kinney
*   *Anne Frank's Diary* by Anne Frank

Talk about it!

There are two learning lines that talk can explore in this activity: first, securing understanding of the difference between past and present tense; and, second, developing understanding of how the two tenses work in diary writing.

*   To secure understanding of tense, use the spatial movement to THEN and NOW areas to draw attention to the distinction between events that are happening now and events that have already happened. If children move to the wrong area, use this as an opportunity to question their reasoning about tense. Your questions might include the following.

» Explain to me why you think it is a THEN event?

» Are you sure about your choice? Tell us what you are thinking?

» Can you change the verb to make it tell us about something that is happening now (or then)?

- To develop understanding of how tense is used in diaries is the most important learning to draw from this activity as it links grammatical understanding with purpose and effect in writing. The use of colour coding is very helpful in facilitating talk as it clarifies where the two tenses are used. You might invite children to think about the following.

» All the past tense verbs are coloured red. Can you see any pattern in what they are talking about?

» Why do you think a diary writer needs to move between past and present tense?

» Let's look at the present-tense verbs. How are they being used in the diary?

» Can you explain how you would shift between past and present if you were writing a diary?

Notes for teachers

1. For Year 2 children, for whom past and present tense are required terminology for them to understand, focus simply on securing their understanding of the different time frames of past and present. With older children, focus more on developing understanding of the different roles that past and present play in a diary — to narrate and to comment/reflect.

2. Where possible, choose extracts that use simple past- and present-tense verb phrases for younger children or children who need support. For higher-level understanding, include some complex verb phrases that require more thought about tense.

Games box

Verbal card sort: Create a set of small cards, each with one verb on it. The verbs should include a range of modal, auxiliary and lexical verbs. Hand out the cards to pairs, and ask them to sort them into three groups: modal, lexical and auxiliary.

Tackling misconceptions

1. The most significant misconception that many children hold is that a verb is a 'doing' word, which really only works well as a definition for very 'active' lexical verbs. Avoid using this definition and instead build children's understanding of how verb phrases are built, including modal verbs and auxiliary verbs. Also make sure that all children understand the verbs *be* and *have* in all their forms.

2.   Another very reasonable misunderstanding is that children think any word that seems to denote an action is a verb (partly because of the misconception above). So, very often, they will identify a noun or an adjective as a verb when what is described is an action. For example, in the sentence 'The hunting was fierce', many children will identify hunting as the verb when it is a noun. Encourage children to recognise that words change their grammatical function depending on where they are in a sentence.

Answers

> The nice thing about Matilda **was** that if you <u>had **met**</u> her casually and <u>**talked**</u> to her you <u>would have **thought**</u> she **was** a perfectly normal five-and-a-half-year-old child. She **displayed** almost no outward signs of her brilliance and she never <u>**showed off**</u>. 'This **is** a very sensible and quiet little girl' you <u>would have **said**</u> to yourself. And unless for some reason you <u>had **started**</u> a discussion with her about literature or mathematics, you <u>would never have **known**</u> the extent of her brain-power.

- All the verb phrases are underlined: simple ones have just a lexical verb and complex ones have auxiliaries as well.
- All the lexical verbs are bold.
- Three of the complex verb phrases include the modal verb *would*.
- Did you notice the adverb *never* in the middle of the last verb phrase? Adverbs are very mobile and can often appear in this position; the most common adverb of all in this position is *not*.

This is not just about identifying grammar: if you look closely at this passage, you will see that the simple verb phrases tend to describe Matilda, whereas the complex verb phrases are all when Dahl invites us as readers to think about what we might have thought about Matilda if we had met her.

3

The noun group

What you need to know

Most of us are confident that, however challenged we are by grammar, we can at least identify nouns. They can, however, be difficult to recognise, especially when they don't refer to 'things'. In fact, the word 'things' is itself a noun that carries a level of abstraction that might make it a difficult noun for a child to identify.

Ask any school child how they might improve their writing and their most common answer will be to say that it needs more description; press them and ask how they might do this, and they will very likely respond that they need to add adjectives. However, adding adjectives before a noun is just one way of creating a noun phrase. This chapter will consider the variety of ways a noun phrase might be expanded to add descriptive detail to a head noun. Nouns and noun phrases are important building blocks of sentences and are flexible, versatile constructions that allow writers to give or withhold detail for their readers.

A note about adjectives

Adjectives are words that express some feature or quality of a noun. This definition stands in contrast to the more common definition that an adjective is a describing word. Pointing out the relationship between the adjective and the noun is key, because lots of words can be descriptive, including adverbs, which add detail to a verb, or indeed any well-chosen noun or verb.

Understanding nouns and noun phrases

Types of noun

A common definition of a noun is that it is a word to name a person, place, thing or idea. People, places and objects can be much easier to recognise than those 'things' and 'ideas' that present a level of abstraction. Consider, for example, the nouns underlined in this extract from William Nicholson's book, *The Wind Singer*. Which nouns are likely to cause problems for children to identify? Which ones might you have missed, and how do *you* know that they are nouns?

> The <u>tower</u> had no obvious <u>purpose</u> of any <u>kind</u>. For a <u>while</u> it was a <u>curios-ity</u>, and the <u>people</u> would stare at it as it creaked this <u>way</u> and that. When the <u>wind</u> blew hard it made a mournful <u>moaning</u> that was comical at <u>first</u> but soon became tiresome.

Another way of thinking about a noun is not to think about what it is, but instead to think about its place, form or function in the sentence. Nouns are likely to have one or more of the following features.

- They *may be* preceded by a determiner (see below for an explanation of a determiner).
  - » All the nouns in the example above are, or could be, preceded by a determiner.
- They *can be* singular or plural.
  - » All the nouns in the example could change from singular to plural (or vice versa) except for 'while' and 'first'.
- They *can be* the subject of the sentence.
  - » '*tower*' is the subject of the first sentence.
- They *can be* the head of a noun phrase (of which more to follow).
  - » For example '*no obvious purpose*'; '*a mournful moaning*'
- There are certain suffixes that, when added to existing words, form nouns (see examples below).
  - » There are two examples in the extract: adding 'ity' to the adjective 'curious' becomes the noun 'curiosity' and adding 'ing' to the noun 'moan' creates another noun — 'moaning'.

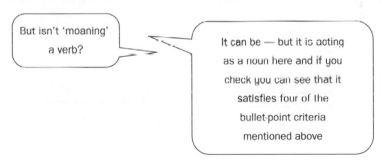

What is a determiner?

Determiners form a small set of words that can be very helpful for recognising nouns because they precede the noun, providing information about:

- quantity (e.g. one, some, many, every, no)

- whether definite or indefinite (the, a)
- ownership (e.g. his, my, your), or
- to single something out (this, that, those, these).

Watch out, though, because sometimes the determiner and the noun can be separated by an adjective — for example, 'a mournful moaning'.

Nouns can be classified as being of six different, sometimes overlapping, types. Knowing about these different types can also help in identifying nouns that are tricky to spot.

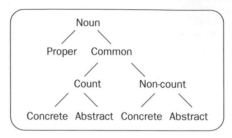

The difference between proper and common nouns is that proper nouns are the particular names of a more general category, for example: Exeter (proper noun) is a city (common noun); Marmite (proper noun) is a food (common noun); Voldemort (proper noun) is a villain (common noun). Proper nouns are capitalised, rarely take plural forms, and are rarely preceded by a determiner (i.e. we don't say 'the Exeter' or 'some Voldemort').

All common nouns can be either count or non-count nouns. Count nouns are individual countable entities that can therefore be plural, but in the singular, rarely appear alone without a determiner. Non-count nouns refer to an undifferentiated mass or notion such as *science, music, hockey* or *advice*; they are rarely plural and can appear without a determiner. This means that both proper nouns and non-count nouns do not generally conform to the first two criteria offered in the earlier bullet-point list, but they do conform to the second two.

Football: the game is a non-count noun, but **a** football is a count noun (see table).

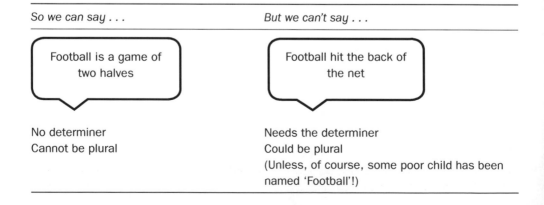

So we can say . . .	But we can't say . . .
Football is a game of two halves	Football hit the back of the net
No determiner Cannot be plural	Needs the determiner Could be plural (Unless, of course, some poor child has been named 'Football'!)

Both count and non-count nouns can be further described as either concrete (visible and measurable) or abstract (conceptual or unobservable notions such as *difficulty*, *kindness* and *amazement*).

Suffixes that form nouns

A **suffix** is an 'ending' used at the end of one word to turn it into another. Understanding the suffixes that form nouns can help with the identification of nouns, and also helps children to recognise how words are built (and indeed how new words are often invented). The table below (taken from Crystal, 2004: 117) illustrates some of the range of suffixes that create nouns.

Abstract nouns		Concrete nouns	
Suffix	Example	Suffix	Example
-age	mileage	-ant	contestant
-al	refusal	-ee	divorcee
-ation	documentation	-er	cricketer
-dom	martyrdom	-ese	Chinese
-(c)ry	bravery	-ess	waitress
-ful	spoonful	-ette	launderette
-hood	childhood	-(i)an	grammarian
-ing	hunting	-ist	socialist
ism	idealism	-ite	socialite
-ment	embarrassment	let	piglet
-ness	sadness	-ling	duckling
-ship	friendship	-or	survivor
		-ster	gangster

But be careful — just because a word *can* be an abstract noun doesn't mean it always is. Consider these two sentences:

1. I remember my childhood fondly. (abstract noun)
2. She was my childhood friend. (adjective)

Another strategy for identifying nouns is to replace a word that you think might be a noun with another word you know is a noun and see if it still makes sense. In *The Wind Singer* example above, we were not sure about the word 'while' until we realised we could replace it with the word 'day' so the extract now read 'For a day it was a curiosity'. This convinced us that, because the two words were serving the same function in the sentence, they must both be nouns.

The noun phrase

A **noun phrase** is a noun and any words added to qualify or add more information about that noun. A **pronoun**, which is a word standing in the place of a noun — such as *it, she, him, they, them, something* — can also form a noun phrase. The noun that all the rest of the noun phrase describes is called the **head noun**. A noun phrase can be as short as a single noun or quite long. You will encounter noun phrases in all texts, not only in descriptive writing. In the examples below, illustrating different genres, the head noun has been underlined for you.

- **On menus**: A crumbly goats' cheese <u>tart</u>, lying on a bed of wilted leaves
- **In promotional material**: An engaging family <u>saga</u> played out in a credible domestic setting, adding up to a thumping good yarn
- **In science**: A colourless <u>gas</u>, giving off a strong choking smell and soluble in water
- **In sports writing**: A real 'Roy of the Rovers' <u>goal</u>, crushing their opponents in the closing minutes of the game
- **In politics**: A true-blue <u>Conservative</u>, with only a touch of the old Etonian
- **In Earth sciences**: The damaging <u>concentrations</u> of 'greenhouse gases' in the Earth's atmosphere

One thing you might notice is that these extended noun phrases can include shorter noun phrases within them. Here are some from the examples above; you should be able to find others.

- A thumping good **yarn**
- The closing **minutes** of the **game**
- The **Earth's atmosphere**

This can be confusing, so it is important to remember that a noun phrase has a head noun — the noun everything else is describing — but other noun phrases can be used to describe that head noun. You can always take out the additional noun phrases and strip the noun phrase back to its head noun:

- An engaging family <u>saga</u> played out in a credible domestic setting, adding up to a thumping good yarn
- An engaging family <u>saga</u> played out in a credible domestic setting
- An engaging family <u>saga</u>
- A <u>saga</u>

A noun phrase is a 'chunk' of a sentence and cannot form a sentence on its own as it needs a finite verb to complete it. Finite verbs that might complete some of the examples above include those highlighted below.

- A crumbly goats' cheese tart, lying on a bed of wilted leaves <u>was</u> the highlight of the menu

- A true-blue Conservative, with only a touch of the old Etonian <u>would</u> be an ideal candidate in the Home Counties
- The damaging concentrations of 'greenhouse gases' in the Earth's atmosphere <u>are</u> now well above their pre-industrial levels

It is often a well-chosen noun phrase that communicates the character of a text as typical of science writing or of a high-class restaurant menu. Pointing them out in a model text or generating them in preparation for writing might be as valuable as a focus on individual words.

The noun in a noun phrase can be **premodified** or **postmodified**, i.e. detail can come *before* (premodified) or *after* the noun (postmodified). Children are much more familiar with premodification, so it is worth drawing attention to other noun phrase patterns. The noun phrase generator presented in the table below allows you to generate quite a variety of extended noun phrases, and includes many of the possible patterns for pre- and postmodification.

There are many structures that can postmodify a noun, but the noun phrase generator uses four very common ones: adjectives; the relative clause; the non-finite clause; and the prepositional phrase. For more explanation about non-finite and relative clauses, have a look at Chapter 5. A **prepositional phrase** is a phrase that starts with a preposition, such as *in, on, under, of* or *for*. A preposition indicates a relationship between two elements in the sentence — often a relationship of time (when) and space (where). For example, 'he sat **in** the background' and 'we met **at** the weekend'. However, other relationships can be expressed, such as 'a woman **of** huge significance'. In a prepositional phrase, the preposition is followed by a noun phrase (including a pronoun). So, again, this is a reminder of the potentially confusing fact that a noun phrase can be modified by a prepositional phrase, which has a noun phrase within it!

The noun phrase generator

Determiner	Adjective(s)	Noun	Adjective(s) Adverb plus adjective	Prepositional phrase	Relative clause	Non-finite clause
The	playful	**teacher**	clearly old	of . . .	who . . .	reminding . . .
Any	forgotten	**dance**	short but memorable	with . . .	that . . .	moving . . .
This	ridiculous	**game**	hilarious and unusual	at . . .	which . . .	beginning . . .

You can be playful with this by trying to generate the longest noun phrase you can create without using the main verb. Here is one possibility:

<u>The newly inspired writing **teacher**, with an eye for detail, clearly knowledgeable, moving around the classroom, making observations that draw attention to noun phrases in the text</u> loved [finite verb] reading what the children had written.

The extract in the box below, from Jane Hissey's *Old Bear*, includes a variety of noun phrases, which have been underlined with the head noun in bold, but every one of the phrases can be mapped using the noun phrase generator that follows.

In the **corner** of the playroom was a little wooden **aeroplane** with a propeller that went round and round. 'We could use this **plane** to get to the **trapdoor**' said **Bramwell**. 'Rather dangerous, I know, but quite honestly I can't bear to think of **Old Bear** up there alone for a **moment** longer.' 'I'll be pilot' said **Rabbit**, hopping up and down, making aeroplane noises.

(Jane Hissey, *Old Bear*)

Determiner	Adjective(s)	Noun	Adjective(s) Adjective plus adverb	Prepositional phrase	Relative clause	Non-finite clause
The		corner		of the playroom		
A	little wooden	aeroplane		with a propeller	that went round and round	
this		plane				
the		trap-door				
		Bramwell				
		Old Bear				
A		moment	longer			
		pilot				
		Rabbit				hopping up and down, making aeroplane noises

Often children are taught to create noun phrases by adding adjectives before the noun. Although, of course, this is a perfectly valid choice, it is unhelpful if children think that noun phrases are only about adjectives before the noun. Sometimes they need to think more about using fewer adjectives and making a better choice of noun. For example, why describe a dog as 'a big, fierce, brown slobbering dog' when you can express that very economically by writing 'A Rottweiler'? So rather than always asking young writers to add more adjectives to create description, you could ask them to look at their noun phrases with adjectives and see if they can choose a more precise noun.

When we speak, we very rarely use adjectives *after* a noun: if we were telling a friend about someone's hands, we might well say 'She had long white fingers' but not 'She had fingers, long and white'. This is a more literary pattern, and by putting the adjectives after the noun, somehow our attention is drawn more to the adjectives than the noun. In *Arthur, High King of Britain*, Michael Morpurgo introduces Guinevere, playing a harp, using this technique:

Her fingers plucked effortlessly. It was her fingers, long, white and dancing, that I loved first. Her hair was the colour of honey, of gold washed in milk. It fell over her face so that I could not see her.

A child might well have written this as 'Her fingers **were** long, white and dancing', which is the more common pattern. Of course, neither version is incorrect, each merely represents a choice. Being aware of this choice yourself means you can point out the difference. Encouraging children to hear the difference such choices make to a text by speaking them out loud might help them to gain an awareness of the relationship between grammar choices and meaning, or between grammar choices and effect.

Teaching activities

What's in a name? Proper nouns and simple noun phrases that focus on appearance to create character

Learning objective: To understand how carefully chosen names, and even very brief descriptions, can create a visual impression and imply character

This lesson considers how a writer might choose a name for a character and how this name can infer ideas about personality. This might work well for any age group; the text you use however might reflect the age group you are working with. This example uses a text for younger children.

Read *Hairy Maclary from Donaldson's Dairy* by Lynley Dodd, which includes the following 'doggie' characters:

- Schnitzel von Krumm with a very low tum
- Bitzer Maloney all skinny and bony
- Muffin McClay like a bundle of hay
- Bottomley Potts covered in spots
- Hercules Morse as big as a horse
- Hairy Maclary from Donaldson's Dairy.

Each dog is described with a noun phrase that is constructed by a very distinctive name (a proper noun) followed by a description that creates a visual impression or additional information. The book also includes characterful images of each dog.

Divide the class into six groups and ask each group to talk about a different dog, considering what kind of a dog they think each one is. You might support their thinking with questions such as:

- What does this dog like doing?
- Where does this dog like to be?
- What does this dog not like doing?
- Does this dog remind you of a character in a book, or on the TV?

Before the groups feed back, ask each group to decide if the name suits the dog and why/why not.

Explain that choosing a name can help a writer show what a character is like; prepare PowerPoint slides or pictures of obvious examples such as Severus Snape, Dumbledore and Voldemort from the *Harry Potter* books. Alternatively, if appropriate, you might choose characters from a book they have recently read.

Hairy Maclary combines a well-chosen name with descriptive postmodification. Look for examples of noun phrases in favourite classroom texts that help create a visual image of a character. For example, take a look at the following extract from *Three Little Wolves and the Big Bad Pig* by Eugene Tivizas, illustrated by Helen Oxenbury.

Once upon a time there were <u>three cuddly little **wolves** with soft fur and fluffy tails who lived with their mother</u>. The first was black, the second was grey and the third was white.

For examples such as this, you could consider suitable names for the little wolves that match the description, developing understanding of proper nouns and the descriptive power of naming. Prepare a set of images of a group that all have something in common, such as dogs, cats, mythical creatures or toys, for example, but within this group ensure that the characters are all different from one another. Give the children time to generate names for the characters, then share ideas about different names for the same character. Finally, ask the children to create a noun phrase using the character's name, plus further description about each of the characters. They can use *Hairy Maclary* for different patterns or draw from any model text you have chosen. This might be a good time to remind the class about proper nouns and capital letters.

For the plenary, compare the different names and visual detail that have been chosen to describe the same characters.

Talk about it!

There are two forms of talk in this lesson — one focusing on generating ideas and the other on explaining the choices of proper nouns matched to visual descriptions.

- Generating ideas: even something as simple as a name needs time and plenty of opportunity to hear other children's ideas. Use this time to:
  » generate lots of alternatives in order to create choice
  » adapt and build on suggested choices
  » contrast different suggestions, pointing out similarities and differences
  » comment on how different names create different impressions.
- Explaining choices: these names and descriptions have been chosen to suggest character and so important support questions might be:
  » Does the name match the description?
  » Will the reader know what kind of character this is? Why?
  » Can you convey the same idea using fewer words? Which words matter?
  » Your character seems slow and careful — how have you made me see that?

Notes for teachers

1. The aim is to make the link between word choice and effect; in this case the choice of a name might be as important as the choice of the adjectives or prepositional phrases chosen to add detail. Asking children to close their eyes and bring the character to mind using only the words draws attention to the fact that words can stand in the place of images in order to create a visual impression. It is this attention to detail that weaker writers, of all ages, struggle with.

2. There is always the danger that we try to do too many things in a single lesson. The text examples here illustrate several features of the noun phrase — the Three Little Wolves extract, for example, includes a determiner, two premodifying adjectives, and both a prepositional phrase and a relative clause postmodifying the noun. However, there is no need to draw explicit attention to all of this in the lesson. The patterns are there to model writing, but the learning focus here is on proper nouns and the creation of visual detail, so don't get lost in the grammar that might have been covered.

Extraordinary and unexpected things: Painting pictures with noun phrases

Learning objective: To understand that a writer can help a reader to visualise an idea through the use of noun phrases

Begin with pictures of natural phenomena in which we often see other things — for example, flames, clouds, patterns in tree bark. With talk partners, ask the children to explain what they see; does everyone see the same thing? If it is a cloudy day you might find somewhere outside where the children can lie down and look up to see what shapes they can see in the clouds. Alternatively, you might bring in artefacts that create the same effect.

Together make a list of all the shapes they have seen, either in the pictures, the artefact or from looking at the sky. As ideas are suggested, you might push for alternative nouns — so you might, for example, look for more precision (leopard or kitten rather than cat), or for more detail ('frightened face' rather than just 'face').

Read the following extract from *The Tender Moments of Saffron Silk* by Glenda Millard:

> One of the most interesting living people Saffron knew was her daddy, because of his ability to see things that other people could not. Extraordinary and unexpected things like mermaidenly ladies in driftwood branches, wild horses rearing from red gum fence posts, wings in wire coat-hangers and angels in the cabbage patch.

There are four noun phrases that describe what Saffron's daddy sees. He sees:

1.   mermaidenly ladies in driftwood branches
2.   wild horses rearing from red gum fence posts
3.   wings in wire coat-hangers
4.   angels in the cabbage patches.

The first two noun phrases are more developed than the last two. In the first two, the writer has added an adjective before the noun and in the second phrase she has followed the noun with a non-finite clause. For the first phrase she has even invented an adjective to describe the ladies in driftwood. Spend some time thinking about these choices. Ask the children to close their eyes and imagine how different choices here change what they imagine. For example:

*   proud ladies in driftwood branches
*   athletic ladies in driftwood branches
*   dinner ladies in driftwood branches!!!

Discuss how, in the second example, 'wild' and 'rearing' seem to go together. Alternatives can also be imagined or visualised:

*   old horses plodding from red gum fence posts
*   racehorses galloping from red gum fence posts
*   fairground horses dancing from red gum fence posts.

In pairs, ask the children to develop the last two noun phrases following the same patterns. These might be imagined in a similar manner to the other examples. The aim is to show how the details of the noun phrase can create an image in the mind's eye, illustrating that information experienced visually needs to be conveyed in words in writing.

The children can then select a few of the shapes seen in the clouds, pictures or artefacts to write a short description of what they saw. It might begin 'Today I have seen extraordinary and unexpected things like . . .'

Talk about it!

Two forms of classroom talk are used in this lesson: the first is the more usual sharing of ideas and generating material to write about. The second is oral rehearsal — hearing written text out loud to evaluate its effect. Encourage the children to try out several different possibilities before choosing one. As you talk with them about their choices you might ask:

- Why did you choose that adjective — what did you want the reader to see?
- Why have you changed your mind — why is this a better choice of 'ing' verb?
- Perhaps there is a stronger noun you might use?
- When you read it out loud, does it make you think of precisely what you saw?
- What do you want the reader to feel about what you saw?

Notes for teachers

1. This lesson draws attention to only two possible patterns for the noun phrase: a pre-modifying adjective and a non-finite clause. The model text itself also includes prepositional phrases as part of the noun phrase. This modest selection from the variety of possibilities the noun phrase offers is deliberate. Children need time to become familiar with the pattern and to play with the possibilities it offers. In order to plan for progression, you will need to ensure that, over time, children encounter all possible patterns and that you return frequently to those you have addressed already. As you slowly address all the possibilities presented by the noun phrase, have a clear focus and purpose each time and don't try to cover too much. The aim is that, in their own writing, the frequent exposure to these common patterns will sensitise them to patterns other than the premodifying adjective — although remember that this is a perfectly sound choice.

2. One possible drawback of explicitly pointing out these patterns is that they become features to deploy — 'I haven't used a relative clause in a while. Better use one now — that will make my teacher happy' — and not a means of expressing what they want to say. The focus on talk about choices is aimed to constantly reinforce the relationship between grammatical choices and authorial intention. So the aim is not 'Can I use a relative clause?' but rather 'Is a relative clause what I need here to better express what I want to say?'

Games box

Invent a menu: Using a real menu as a model, invent a menu using noun phrases for characters such as Fungus the Bogeyman, Winnie-the-Pooh, a giant from the BFG (or any character likely to have an interesting diet!).

Noun phrase builder: This can be changed every few weeks to match a class topic. Choose a character or a place from a book the class is reading, or a focus for a science or geography topic, and create sort cards to build noun phrases. Colour-code the different elements — e.g. blue cards for determiners, green for adjectives, white for the head noun (this might be in larger bold font), pink for relative clauses, beige for non-finite clauses, purple for prepositional phrases — over the course of the topic children can add to the cards using the colour-coding. Different phrases can be built and attached to a poster picturing the head noun.

Surprising nouns: Set a challenge to find the most surprising nouns. This might run for a few weeks and contributions can be added to a wall chart. The wall chart might include clues such as:

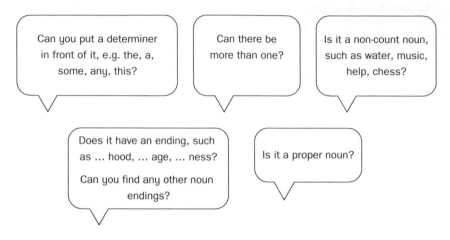

Tackling misconceptions

1. A noun phrase is part of a sentence, not a complete sentence in its own right, but because children are often taught that a sentence makes sense on its own, they sometimes think a noun phrase is a sentence (because it does make sense on its own). Be aware of this when teaching about noun phrases, and regularly encourage children to complete their noun phrases with a finite verb. For example, if you were looking at the noun phrase *a little wooden* **aeroplane** *with a propeller that went round and round,* from *Old Bear,* you could help children to create complete sentences where the noun phrase is at the beginning of the sentence or at the end of the sentence, before or after a finite verb:

    A little wooden **aeroplane** with a propeller that went round and round lay on my window sill.

    I had a little wooden **aeroplane** with a propeller that went round and round.

2. One challenging aspect of English grammar is that a word can be a noun in one sentence, a verb in another and an adjective in another. Rather than waiting for this to cause confusion, draw attention to it when appropriate. The example of *moaning* noted earlier in this chapter is a good one to play with:

It made a mournful <u>moaning</u> (noun: it is preceded by a determiner and an adjective)

I heard a <u>moaning</u> sound (adjective: it is giving more information about the noun sound)

He was <u>moaning</u> with pain (verb: it is describing what he is doing, and is a lexical verb).

3. Be aware yourself of the nested nature of grammar. Many people learning grammar believe that there is a single label for a structure, such as a noun phrase, in a sentence, but often there are multiple layers, as this chapter has shown. Remember, a prepositional phrase has a noun phrase in it and a noun phrase can have a prepositional phrase in it!

Noun phrase: <u>three cuddly little **wolves** with soft fur and fluffy tails who lived with their mother</u>

Prepositional phrase: <u>with soft fur and fluffy tails</u>

Noun phrases: <u>soft fur</u>; <u>fluffy tails</u>.

4

The adverb group

Grammar joke

Q: What five-letter word becomes shorter when you add two letters to it?
A: Short

What you need to know

The adverb is probably the most versatile and flexible word class in English. It is tempting to see adverbs as the counterpart to adjectives and assume that they modify verbs much as adjectives modify nouns. However, they actually play a much wider variety of roles. Their core function is to modify — not just verbs, but also adjectives, pronouns, other adverbs, phrases, clauses or even whole sentences. In this chapter, we focus on explaining the different functions of adverbs, and the different types of phrases and clauses that can act as adverbials. While adverbs have a bad reputation in creative writing circles (see Stephen King's famous quotation, 'The road to hell is paved with adverbs') you'll see in this chapter that adverbials — any group of words that performs the function of an adverb — are a rich resource for building detail, and their flexible positioning within a sentence lends itself to experimentation and play. We will also look at the 'connectives problem' — the difference between conjunctions and sentence adverbs — which is a common cause of confusion for children.

Understanding adverbs

The function of adverbs

Starred (*) examples in this section and the next come from *The Queen's Knickers* by Nicholas Allen.

The key function of an adverb is to modify another element of a sentence; in fact, aside from nouns (which are modified by adjectives), they can modify almost every other word type:

* verb (*traditionally* decorated)*
* adverb (She sang *extremely* loudly)

- adjective (*slightly* smaller)*
- pronoun (*nearly* everyone).

Adverbs can also modify whole clauses, phrases or even sentences:

- I spotted *only* one crocodile (*only* modifies the noun phrase *one crocodile*)
- We made it *almost* to the end (*almost* modifies the prepositional phrase *to the end*)
- No one can see them *anyway** (*anyway* modifies the sentence as a whole).

Categories of adverb

Adverbs are categorised according to the type of additional information they provide; sometimes this is described as 'What question do they answer?' They are such a large and diverse class of words that you will be able to find several different ways of classifying them, but some of the most commonly used categories are shown in the table below.

Category	Question	Example
Time	When	They were *first* worn by Queen Victoria.* We came *yesterday*.
Place	Where	We waited *below*. They got *everywhere*.
Manner	How	The Queen likes to dress *smartly*.* They are a gift from Scandinavia and are *traditionally* decorated with real holly.*
Reason	Why	No one can see them *anyway*.* *Therefore*, I decided to take the shorter route.
Degree	How much	She keeps her Christmas message *very* short.* They . . . are *rather* baggy.* It was *only just* sorted out.*

-ly words

The idea that adverbs are -ly words stems from the fact that one large group of adverbs is formed by adding -ly to adjectives, often to form adverbs of manner: *carefully, tentatively, happily, ecstatically, hungrily, ravenously*, and so on. However, using this as a way to identify adverbs can be misleading. Several new suffixes that form adverbs have been introduced in modern English. Sometimes, hyphens show that these are new coinages, but many have become assimilated into our language as single words. These include:

-like; -wise; -style; -ways

e.g. in workmanlike; businesslike; school-wise; American-style; sideways.

In addition, there are other large groups of adverbs that aren't formed in these ways, including the following.

- Many time adverbs: *later, never, often, once, soon, today, tomorrow, yesterday.*
- Many place adverbs: *here, there, everywhere.*
- Many degree adverbs: *almost, just, quite.*

It's also important to note that there are other types of word that end in 'ly', including the following.

- Adjectives: *lovely, deadly, jolly, lonely.*
- Nouns: *bully, holly, jelly, family.*
- Verbs: *bully, multiply, apply, supply.*

Consequently, it is often unhelpful to provide children with a definition that focuses on the 'ly' suffix as a key feature of adverbs, though it can be a useful starting point to teach them that one big group of adverbs end with -ly.

Conjuncts (sentence-level adverbs)

The term 'connective' is used to refer to a variety of words and phrases, some of which function in very different ways. This can lead to confusion for children (and teachers!). Some of what we call 'connectives' are actually conjuncts, a type of adverb that links ideas across independent grammatical units: finite clauses, sentences or paragraphs. Others are conjunctions (an entirely separate word class); these join clauses or parts of clauses together within a sentence, through co-ordination or subordination.

Conjuncts include words that:

- list — *first, second, finally*
- add — *furthermore, moreover*
- contrast — *however, alternatively*
- sum up — *overall, in conclusion*
- show a result — *consequently, therefore*
- shift attention — *meanwhile, incidentally.*

Conjunct or conjunction?

A good way to show the difference between conjuncts and conjunctions is to look at the difference between *however* and *although.* Both of these words have a similar purpose in that they create a contrast and show that one thing doesn't necessarily lead to another.

The conjunct adverb *however* can be used to link ideas across two entirely separate sentences, as follows.

- It was raining. *However*, we still went out.
- It was raining. We, *however*, still went out.

If you want to create a single sentence using *however*, it is common to use a semicolon:

- It was raining; we, *however*, still went out.

In contrast, the conjunction *although* automatically requires the two ideas it joins to be within a single sentence, as it subordinates one clause to the other:

- We went out *although* it was raining.
- *Although* it was raining, we still went out.

Disjuncts

A final type of adverb that it's useful to know about is the disjunct. These are adverbs that are used to comment on a whole clause or sentence, standing apart from it:

- *Surprisingly*, he didn't want any cake.
- *Honestly*, I can't tell you.
- It's not open today, *apparently*.

Understanding adverbials

While an adverb is a single word, an adverbial is a string of words that performs the same function. Adverbials may be phrases or clauses. They always have a modifying function, and they can usually be replaced by an adverb (e.g. 'Before we left, we had one last drink'/'Beforehand, we had one last drink'). All of the types of adverb described above, including conjuncts and disjuncts, can take the form of a string of words.

Four common types of adverbial are *prepositional phrases, noun phrases, subordi- nate clauses* and *non-finite clauses*.

Prepositional phrases

These adverbials begin with a preposition:

- He found the truants *at home*.
- Her narrative plots are completely *over the top*.

A great example of the use of adverbial prepositional phrases is *Rosie's Walk* by Pat Hutchings. The written narrative is a single sentence created almost entirely from adverbial prepositional phrases, while the pictures that accompany it tell a much richer story of a fox stalking the hen, getting into all sorts of trouble:

> Rosie the hen went for a walk, across the yard, around the pond, over the haycock . . .

Noun phrases

These adverbials have a noun as their head:

* Jane telephoned me *last night*.
* *Tomorrow morning*, we'll go to the park.

Subordinate clauses

These adverbials are finite clauses linked to the main clause with a subordinating conjunction:

* *If you work hard,* you'll pass.
* She ran *as fast as she could.*
* John knew *when he was beaten.*

Non-finite clauses

These have non-finite verbs as their head:

* *Slipping on the icy surface*, the boy grabbed hold of my hand.
* Open the door *to let the cat out.*
* *To be honest*, I can't tell which is which.

Adverbials in action

To see the impact and importance of adverbials, we can look at this short extract from *The Reptile Room* by Lemony Snicket. The adverbials are underlined, and finite verbs in the main clauses are in bold:

> Jumping to her feet, Violet **sprinted** back into the house as if Stephano were already after her and **pushed** her way through the door into the kitchen. Shoving a chair to the floor in her haste, she **grabbed** a bar of soap from the dripping sink. She **rubbed** the slippery substance carefully over her lockpick until the entire invention had a thin, slick coating. Her heart pounding in her chest, she **ran** back outside, taking a hurried look through the walls of the Reptile Room.

If you remove the adverbials from this passage, this is what you get:

> Violet **sprinted** . . . and **pushed** her way . . . she **grabbed** a bar of soap . . . she **rubbed** the slippery substance . . . she **ran**

The stripped-down narrative doesn't quite make sense; however, it might look grammatically quite similar to the type of narrative writing that some of your children are doing, with a focus on fast-paced events happening sequentially, the 'then . . . and then . . . and then . . .' approach. What's really interesting here is that it's not an abundance of adverbs and adjectives that create the full and detailed image conveyed in the full version. There are few adverbs ('back', 'carefully', 'outside') and a handful of adjectives ('dripping', 'slippery', 'entire', 'thin, slick', 'hurried'). Rather, the passage is full of adverbials that describe *how* and *where* Violet's activities are occurring.

The pattern of the main clauses is actually rather repetitive, particularly because of the repeated pronoun 'she grabbed . . . she rubbed . . . she ran'. The rhythm and variety of this passage is created by the adverbial detail, particularly the pattern of non-finite clauses acting as adverbials — 'jumping', 'shoving', 'pounding' — headed by verbs (present participles) that suggest dramatic action.

Here's a breakdown of the adverbials in the passage.

Non-finite subordinate clause	Jumping to her feet Shoving a chair to the floor in her haste Her heart pounding in her chest taking a hurried look
Finite subordinate clause	as if Stephano were already after her until the entire invention had a thin, slick coating
Prepositional phrase	into the house through the door into the kitchen from the dripping sink over her lockpick through the walls of the Reptile Room
Adverb	back, carefully, outside

Adverbials are also important to add specificity and detail to the information given in non-fiction texts. The following two sentences from a Children's encyclopedia show how much of the content of many sentences is conveyed through adverbials. Have a go at identifying where the adverbials are (answers at the end of the chapter).

'Boxing Kangaroos' in *Children's A to Z Encyclopedia*, Miles Kelley

Male kangaroos push, pull and wrestle with their arms, and may kick out with their great feet, using their strong tail for support. They are battling for females at breeding time.

Adverbial mobility

One of the features of adverbials is their mobility within a sentence. They can appear before a clause, in the middle of a clause and after a clause. This makes them ideal for experimentation and play.

Positions of adverbials

Before the clause:

- *Chatting on the telephone,* he crossed the road.
- *Although I couldn't see anything,* I could hear the train whistle.
- *Last night* I saw a shooting star.

After the clause:

- We went *to the beach.*
- I danced, *swaying rhythmically with the music.*
- We'll see you *tomorrow.*

In the middle of a clause:

- I thought that, *even though I haven't tried it myself,* you might like it.
- The monkeys were *playfully* jumping.
- They had, *to be fair,* done their best.

Adverbials can also be chained together almost endlessly to create extremely long sentences:

> Despite the snow lying outside in drifts almost 6 feet deep, despite the wind howling wildly through the trees, he stoically trudged onwards in the darkness, bowing his head and urging his legs forwards, one after the other.

Teaching activities

Where might we go? Exploring atmosphere with prepositional phrases

Learning objective: Understand how to create atmosphere when describing a journey using prepositional phrases

Start with a series of atmospheric prepositional phrases that can be used as adverbials, perhaps on cards (if you want to extend children you could give them metaphorical phrases):

> by the forgotten river
>
> under the chestnut tree
>
> beyond the sea
>
> over the horizon
>
> in the shadows

> east of the sun,
>
> west of the moon
>
> in the back of beyond
>
> over the rainbow
>
> behind midnight

Ask the children to discuss in pairs what each of these places might be like, what might be happening there, who they might meet there, and to choose their favourite one. Explain that these are all prepositional phrases, and that they can be used to add detail and create atmosphere in a description. Explain that, when they are put with a verb — like 'sitting' or 'flying' — they become adverbial prepositional phrases, explaining where something is happening. Ask them what they chose as their favourite phrase, what the place they imagined is like, and help them to describe the atmosphere of that place.

Select a text that uses adverbial prepositional phrases to create effective detail, and read this with the children. Show them where the phrases are, and then give them the opportunity to try out using phrases in a similar way in their own writing. One text that you could use is *Where the Wild Things Are* by Maurice Sendak.

After reading and discussing the book, display the following short extract:

Max stepped into his private boat and waved goodbye

and sailed back over a year

and in and out of weeks

and almost over a day

and into the night of his very own room

where he found his supper waiting for him

and it was still hot.

Ask them what is happening in this extract, and what the 'feeling' or 'atmosphere' of this extract is. How does it create the feeling that Max is going on a long journey? How does it create the feeling that it is magical?

Then ask children to identify the prepositional phrases, reminding them to look at the examples from the start of the lesson for ideas (*over a year; in and out of weeks; over a day; into the night of his very own room*). Show how these phrases are all describing the verb 'sailed', telling us 'where' Max sailed, how they create a feeling of a long journey by the way that the prepositional phrases are all chained together, and how the feeling of magic is created by the unusual way in which they describe him moving 'in and out of weeks', etc.

Ask children to imagine going on a journey to the place that they created in their starter activity. What might the journey be like? What atmosphere or feeling would that journey have? Choose one example and model how you could write a description of the journey, following the format of Max's voyage but keeping it simple and concrete if necessary, e.g. 'We trekked across the sandy desert, under the cold stars, in and out of dunes, over the barren sea, and into the back of beyond.' As you write, try to verbally model thinking about how the choice of prepositional phrases is creating atmosphere (e.g. loneliness, coldness in this example). Remember to identify a verb at the start (like 'trekked') for their phrases to hook on to.

Ask children, in pairs, to have a go at writing a single sentence describing the journey to their imagined place, following this format. In feedback afterwards, focus on asking them about how they chose phrases and what atmosphere they wanted to create. This could lead in to a more developed piece of writing.

Another text that you could use for this is *The Highwayman* by Alfred Noyes. Here you could look at the repetition of the prepositional phrase 'by moonlight':

> Watch for me by moonlight;
>
> I'll come to thee by moonlight, though hell should bar the way!

Children could then experiment with writing a narrative poem that uses a prepositional phrase as a refrain in this way (possibly one from the starter activity). For an extension task, you could look at the way in which one iteration of 'the moonlight' stops being a prepositional phrase and actually becomes the object of the verb:

> Her musket shattered the moonlight

Children could have a go at following this pattern in their own poem, for example:

We lay beneath the chestnut tree,

we dreamed beneath the chestnut tree,

The wild wind shook the chestnut tree . . .

Talk about it!

This activity relies on talk to help children make the link between the details given in the prepositional phrases and the atmosphere that they create. Talk happens in three key contexts.

1. Paired discussion in the starter activity and in the writing task. This will be exploratory, tentative and focused on generating ideas.
2. Teacher modelling in shared writing activities. Try to model exploration and play as you do this, asking them to come up with different ideas, and using some questioning to draw out the mood/atmosphere/feelings associated with those ideas

before explaining what you're choosing to write and why. 'What do these phrases make you imagine?' 'What picture do they create in your head?' 'What makes them sound magical?' 'How do they make the journey sound long?'

3. Whole-class discussion. Here you will need to clarify their understanding of prepositional phrases, and to use questioning to draw out how the choice of phrase links to atmosphere. You can do this particularly effectively when looking at the examples children have written themselves: 'What did you want your reader to feel about the journey?' 'What picture did you want to create in their head?'

Notes for teachers

1. A list of prepositions would be a useful support for many children: *on, under, behind,* etc. You can show them how these can be developed in to prepositional phrases.

2. Younger or less able children might still like to experiment with the idea that prepositional phrases might be 'magical' or 'imaginative', and don't have to be realistic, as in the *Wild Things* example. To do this, you will need to spend more time just looking at how to create prepositional phrases that are 'magical' by using a preposition in an unusual way, e.g. 'behind the sky', 'under the dream', 'beyond the dawn'.

What are they like? Using adverbial similes

Learning objective: Understand how to create imaginative descriptions using adverbial similes

Start with this section from *The Night Before Christmas*:

> Away to the window
>
> I flew like a flash,
>
> tore open the shutters
>
> and threw up the sash.

Ask children to imagine what they would do if they heard Father Christmas land on the roof of their house. How would they act? What would they be feeling?

Point out the line 'I flew like a flash'. Elicit or explain that this is a simile. Discuss the effect of the line — for example, how fast the short words are, the alliteration of 'f' making it sound exciting. Explain that 'like a flash' is describing the movement.

Show them some more common adverbial similes, and ask them whether they can think of any more. Point out that these are adverbial because they're describing how things are happening (see the support notes for teachers, below).

He ran like the wind.

She danced like a butterfly.

They sang like birds.

We laughed like hyenas.

Explain that adverbial similes can be really useful when describing things because they tell us how things behave — move, act, etc. Read the section of the poem that describes Father Christmas (called St Nicholas in the poem). Discuss what impression we get of him. Then show them these two stanzas:

The stump of a pipe

he held tight in his teeth,

and the smoke, it encircled

his head like a wreath.

He had a broad face,

and a round little belly

that shook when he laughed

like a bowl full of jelly.

Ask them to find the similes. What is being described? (The smoke circling round his head; his belly shaking when he laughs.) What are they being compared to? (A Christmas wreath; a bowl of jelly.) Reinforce that these are adverbial because they're describing not just the smoke but what it is doing, not just the belly but how it is moving. Discuss what makes these similes effective: how do they help us to imagine the scene? A wreath is a circle, and decorative and Christmassy; jelly is fun and used in celebrations, etc.

Ask them to write some adverbial similes that describe someone they know well. Model how to begin and/or give them sentence openings that contain a verb for them to describe:

- My baby brother cries like . . .
- My big sister sings like . . .
- My best friend runs like . . .
- My teacher laughs like . . .

Choose two or three examples and model an explanation of why they are effective, talking about the particular image they create (you could draw this out through questioning with older/more able children). In groups, ask them to choose their favourites and explain why they like them. This could then lead in to longer writing tasks — either a shared composition or individual/pair descriptions or poems.

Talk about it!

Again, talk is crucial for drawing out how these similes have particular effects and create particular impressions of St Nicholas. Teacher modelling and whole-class discussion is used to scaffold children's ability to create similes and to talk about the impact that they have.

*   In whole-class discussion, try to ensure that plenty of time is spent on talking about the effect of the similes, not just explaining how they are adverbial (children will be able to follow the pattern to create the similes even if they don't fully understand the terminology). Ask children what 'picture' and what 'feeling' the similes create — 'How do these descriptions make us feel about St Nicholas?' 'What picture do you get in your head of him?' — or, if they're struggling to articulate effects — 'How does it make him sound Christmassy?' 'How does it make him sound fun and friendly?'

*   This whole-class discussion of effects is also important to scaffold the group discussion where they choose their favourite similes and explain why they like them. You may need to give them some prompts to help — 'What picture does it make you imagine?' 'What feeling does it give you?'

Notes for teachers

1. This might work best once children already have some familiarity with the concept of a 'simile'.

2. The children might offer you similes that aren't adverbial but, rather, just describe a person: 'He is like a wolf.' To help them, focus them on coming up with an action first — something the person is doing — then a simile to describe it: 'He eats like a wolf.' You can model this process, or use sentence stems like the ones given above to help this.

3. As an extension, you can introduce more detail before the simile and see if children can follow a more complex pattern: 'He gobbles the food like a wolf.' 'He runs through the grass like a cheetah.'

4. Consider using images to help children to generate ideas. You could ask them to bring in photos of someone they would like to write about, and use those photos to help them write their similes.

Games box

Conjunct vs conjunction: Give children cards with different finite clauses written on them in green, conjuncts in red and conjunctions in blue. Ask them to see how many different sentences they can make out of the cards, then ask them to work out what the difference is between the types of words on the red and blue cards.

Preposition consequences: Give children slips of paper with a very simple sentence written in the middle, e.g. 'I sat.' Ask them to write a prepositional phrase in front or after it (e.g. 'I sat on the fence'/'Under a tree, I sat'). Tell them to pass the piece of paper on and add another prepositional phrase to the new sentence they have. Keep going until they have the longest sentence they can possibly make. You can do this with other adverbial phrases too (so get them to add non-finite clauses, subordinate clauses, etc.).

Killing adverbs: Ask children to identify the adverbs in a short piece of writing, then remove the adverbs and instead find a stronger way of writing the words that they are modifying (to keep this simple you could just look at adverbs that modify verbs), e.g. 'I walked slowly' becomes 'I dawdled.'

In the manner of: Have a stack of adverbial phrases on cards and give children an action to mime (e.g. playing tennis, walking a dog). Give them one at a time and ask them to mime 'in the style of' that adverbial, with the rest of the class guessing what it is. You can start with simple adverbs (slowly, angrily) and move on to more challenging phrases (in the rain; on top of a tightrope; shivering uncontrollably; while being attacked by wasps).

Where goes the adverbial?: Give children cards with a finite clause on, and some adverbials that can modify that clause. Ask them to try out different positions for the adverbials and choose their favourite, then discuss the effect of the different patterns. (Ideally, do this with an example from a real book you're reading with them so that they can compare their choice to the one made by the author.) For example (using one from earlier):

her heart pounding in her chest	she ran

back outside	taking a hurried look through the walls of the Reptile Room

Tackling misconceptions

-ly words

As mentioned earlier, one common problem is that children end up believing that all adverbs end with the -ly suffix or, conversely, that any word ending in -ly must be an adverb. In one of our studies, for example, we overheard a brilliant example of this confusion when one student explained to another that 'broccoli' must be an adverb 'because it ends in *lee*'.

It makes sense to teach the -ly group of adverbs early on as they are relatively easy, but it's important to avoid saying that 'adverbs end in -ly'. Instead, tell them that 'one big group of adverbs end in -ly', then build knowledge of the other adverbs later.

Conjunct/conjunction confusion

Again, this has been tackled above, but it is common for children in upper primary who have been taught about connectives to make mistakes relating to the different uses of sentence-level adverbs (conjuncts) that link *across* sentences, and conjunctions that link words, phrases and clauses *within* a sentence. If you teach connectives, try to distinguish between those that connect between sentences, and those that connect within sentences. This has implications for punctuation, too, as it relates to sentence boundaries: *It rained. Therefore I took an umbrella. It rained so I took an umbrella.*

Grammatical layering

Children are often confused by the fact that something can be a prepositional phrase *and* an adverbial, or a subordinate clause *and* an adverbial. Try to focus on the fact that you identify a structure as adverbial by its *function*, looking at what it is doing to the rest of the sentence. If it is modifying a verb, adverb or adjective — telling you *how*, *when*, *where*, *why* or *how much* something is happening — then it is adverbial, regardless of what else it might also be.

Answers

Adverbials are underlined. Finite verbs in the main clauses are in bold.

> Male kangaroos **push**, **pull** and **wrestle** <u>with their arms</u>, and **may** kick <u>out</u> <u>with their great feet</u>, <u>using their strong tail for support</u>. They **are** battling <u>for</u> <u>females</u> <u>at breeding time</u>.

Prepositional phrase	with their arms
	with their great feet
	for females
	at breeding time
Non-finite clause	using their strong tail for support*
	*'for support' is a prepositional phrase inside this non-finite clause
Adverb	out

5
Clauses

What you need to know

Understanding more about clauses is the natural next step once you have developed confidence with verbs and verb phrases, nouns and noun phrases, and adverbs and adverbial phrases. Although we often think of words as the 'sub-units' of sentences, in actual fact, one of the real building blocks for sentences is the groups of words called clauses. They are key to understanding the syntax of a sentence. Developmentally, for young writers, a growing control of clauses and a diversity in the way clauses are used in writing are markers of growing maturity as a writer. So clauses are very important. But we know from our research that syntax and clauses are aspects of grammar where many teachers feel less secure. This chapter, therefore, will focus on building more understanding of different types of clauses.

A clause always contains a verb phrase (which, you will remember from Chapter 3, can be a single verb or a complex verb phrase with a string of verbs). Let's look at the opening sentence of three popular children's books. These three sentences each have different verb phrase and clause patterns. Two of them just contain one clause, and one sentence is multiply claused. Can you determine which is which?

'Sophie couldn't sleep.'

(*The BFG*, Roald Dahl)

'Naughty Nigel thought he could do anything he wanted.'

(*Naughty Nigel*, Tony Ross)

'This is Mr Gumpy.'

(*Mr Gumpy's Outing*, John Burningham)

The first step in trying to analyse the clauses in a sentence is to find the verb phrases:

1.   This <u>is</u> Mr Gumpy.
2.   Sophie <u>couldn't sleep</u>.
3.   Naughty Nigel <u>thought</u> he <u>could do</u> anything he <u>wanted</u>.

The opening of *Mr Gumpy's Outing* is a single clause, with a simple verb phrase — 'is'. Similarly, the opening of *The BFG* is also a single clause, although it has a complex verb phrase of two verbs — 'couldn't sleep'. But the opening of *Naughty Nigel* has three clauses in it, which you can see because there are three verb phrases underlined:

Naughty Nigel <u>thought</u>/he <u>could do</u> anything/he <u>wanted</u>.

A clause with only one verb phrase is a simple sentence; but sentences with more than one clause are multiply claused sentences (more about sentences in Chapter 6). So sometimes a clause is a sentence on its own, and sometimes it is part of a sentence.

Understanding co-ordinated clauses

When there is more than one clause in a sentence, the clauses are often (but not always) joined by a **conjunction**, a word or group of words whose function is to be the connectors in a sentence. With co-ordinated clauses, the most common conjunctions used are *and, but* and *or*. The co-ordinating conjunctions link clauses expressing ideas that are equally important in the sentence. A writer could always choose to write each of these clauses as a separate sentence, but this would make the writing sound a little disconnected. Using co-ordinated clauses allows the writer to make choices about which ideas to put together. Let's look again at the opening sections of *Naughty Nigel, The BFG* and *Mr Gumpy's Outing*, each of which makes use of co-ordinated clauses. The verb phrases (all single verbs here) are underlined and the conjunction is in bold type.

Sophie <u>closed</u> her eyes **and** <u>lay</u> quite still.

(*The BFG*, Roald Dahl)

Away he <u>went</u> **and** nobody <u>saw</u> him again until the evening.

(*Naughty Nigel*, Tony Ross)

Mr Gumpy <u>owned</u> a boat **and** his house <u>was</u> by a river.

(*Mr Gumpy's Outing*, John Burningham)

All three of these sentences are just two clauses joined by *and,* probably the simplest way of creating co-ordinated clauses. And, of course, the two clauses can be joined by other co-ordinating conjunctions, such as *but* or *or.* It's worth noting too that sometimes a comma is used instead of *and*, especially when the adverb *then* is the next word. There are examples of both of these in *The BFG* (see below). Sometimes children think *then* is a conjunction, but in a sentence where the comma is acting as the co-ordinator, you can always rewrite the sentence replacing the comma with *and* ('He trotted off for about a hundred yards and then he stopped').

'You <u>might not be thinking</u> it **but** spiders <u>is</u> the most tremendous natterboxes.'

He <u>trotted</u> off for about a hundred yards, then he <u>stopped</u>.

(*The BFG*, Roald Dahl)

However, there can be several co-ordinated clauses in one sentence, especially in narratives where a sequence of actions in the story is described. The oral narrative of the *Three Little Pigs* famously uses the repeated refrain describing the Big Bad Wolf — *He huffed and he puffed and he blew the house down*. This is a sequence of three co-ordinated clauses linked with the conjunction *and*. Usually we would discourage children from having too many clauses joined with *and*, but sometimes the deliberate use of a string of co-ordinated clauses joined with *and* can be effective in conveying a heightened sense of a sequence of actions.

Below are four of many examples from *The BFG* of sentences with more than two co-ordinated clauses. Have a look at them, and think about the effects they create in the telling of the story (and look for where a comma replaces the conjunction *and*).

They punched and kicked and scratched and bit and butted each other as hard as they could.

He rolled and wiggled, he fought and he figgled, he squirmed and he squiggled.

The giants roared and screamed and cursed, and for many minutes the noise of battle rolled across the yellow plain.

He took a deep breath, puffed out his cheeks and then whoof!

(*The BFG*, Roald Dahl)

A word of caution!

We are looking at clauses in this chapter, but conjunctions can join words and phrases too. There is a lovely example in *Mr Gumpy's Outing* of a sentence with two co-ordinated clauses, which includes a very long sequence of noun phrases co-ordinated by *and*. Here you can see that the first clause tells us that Mr Gumpy and the long list of animals swam to the bank, and the second clause tells us they climbed out to dry in the sun.

> Then Mr Gumpy and the goat and the calf and the chickens and the sheep and the pig and the dog and the cat and the rabbit and the children all <u>swam</u> to the bank **and** <u>climbed</u> out to dry in the sun.
>
> (*Mr Gumpy's Outing*, Tony Ross)

Understanding finite subordinate clauses

A subordinate clause is one that is dependent upon, or less important than, the main clause in a sentence, and usually (but not always!) you can remove a subordinate clause without creating any problems of grammar and meaning in the main clause. There are several different kinds of subordinate clause, and in this chapter we are going to deal first with finite subordinate clauses, then we will explore relative clauses, and non-finite clauses, both of which are also subordinate clauses.

Finite subordinate clauses are both very common in written texts and very useful. Through subordination, a writer can provide additional detail and information in a sentence, and express complex relationships between ideas. Just as with co-ordinate clauses, finite subordinate clauses are created through using conjunctions. There are many subordinating conjunctions — some are single-word conjunctions, and some are made up of several words, as illustrated in the diagram below.

when because if as unless that since unless although after until whenever where why how while

even though as long as in order that as soon as so that as though

These subordinators join the subordinate clauses to the main clause in a sentence; very often, a writer can choose whether the subordinate clause should be at the beginning, the middle or the end of the sentence. In the examples below, you can see this variety in position. It's also worth noting how the subordinating conjunction *that* can be left out completely, making it harder to notice that it is a subordinate clause! We have shown the omitted *that* in the examples below by inserting it in square brackets, but it is not there in the texts themselves.

> **When** the BFG had consumed his seventy-second fried egg, Mr Tibbs sidled up to the Queen.
>
> The nine pilots in their helicopters suddenly realised **[that]** they were being left behind.
>
> (*The BFG*, Roald Dahl)

Dawn was just breaking **as** <u>he arrived home</u>.

Nigel was so surprised **[that]** <u>he couldn't think of a single wish</u>.

(Naughty Nigel, Tony Ross)

While there can be only one main clause, there can be several subordinate clauses, so it is possible to create very long and complicated sentences (just have a look at a passage from a Charles Dickens novel!). Young writers may need support in recognising how to manage multiply claused sentences so they can show the relationship between a range of ideas or points in a sentence, without making the sentence confused or hard to understand.

Understanding relative clauses

Relative clauses are also subordinate clauses and they provide more detail or information about a noun. They are one of the grammatical elements that form part of a noun phrase, and always follow the head noun (look back at Chapter 3 to remind yourself about the noun phrase). Relative clauses begin with a relative pronoun, the most common being *who, whom, whose, which, that*. In modern English, the use of *whom* is declining rapidly and is more common in writing than in speech. It is a very formal usage and, increasingly, writers and speakers choose to be less formal and use *who* or *that* instead. It is also a usage that is often formed using a preposition plus the relative pronoun, *whom*, as in the final example below. The relative clause is underlined, the relative pronoun is in bold type, and the noun it is modifying is boxed.

The boxed[boy] **who** <u>lived next door</u> . . .

I saw the boxed[man] **whose** <u>hair I had admired</u>.

The lady held the boxed[bag] of apples **which** <u>I wanted</u>.

I was woken by the boxed[dog] **that** <u>barked incessantly</u>.

Here is the boxed[man] **whom** <u>I was talking to</u>.

*Here is the boxed[man] **with whom** <u>I was talking</u>.*

Below are some examples of relative clauses from *The BFG*. As you look at these examples, think about whether the relative clause is adding extra information about the noun, which could be removed, or whether the information in the relative clause is crucial for clarity.

She reached out for her boxed[glasses] **that** <u>lay on the chair beside her bed</u>.

All of the great boxed[lumps] of snozzcumber **that** <u>were in his mouth</u>, as well as Sophie herself, went shooting across the cave.

But in the end it is the boxed[Meatdripper] **who** <u>is having the picnic</u>.

boxed[Sophie], **who** <u>was also staring into the glass jar</u>, cried out.

Restrictive and non-restrictive relative clauses

The information in a relative clause is either crucial to the sense of the sentence or additional information that could be removed without disrupting the clarity of the meaning of the sentence. When the information is crucial, it is called a **restrictive** relative clause, and **non-restrictive** when the information is not essential. Although this might seem like a rather unnecessary distinction, it is important to avoid ambiguity in writing. David Crystal (2004: 151) gives a lovely example, which shows this clearly:

Snakes <u>which are poisonous</u> should be avoided.

Snakes, <u>which are poisonous</u>, should be avoided.

The first sentence is a restrictive relative clause because the writer is pointing out that it is only poisonous snakes we need to avoid, whereas the second sentence has a non-restrictive relative clause, signalled by the commas, which implies that all snakes should be avoided.

The same is true in the examples below. In the first, the restrictive relative clause, the information about the girl's red hair distinguishes her from other girls with different hair colours and helps specify precisely which girl grabbed the man. In the second, the non-restrictive clause, the information about the hair colour is additional and could be left out.

The girl <u>who had red hair</u> grabbed the man.

The girl, <u>who had red hair</u>, grabbed the man.

Understanding non-finite clauses

Another group of clauses to consider are the non-finite clauses, which begin with a non-finite verb. Like relative clauses, these are also always subordinate clauses, and they are very commonly used in both writing and speech. They are very useful clauses because they can convey additional detail and information economically in fewer words than using the full finite version. Have a look at the examples below from *The BFG* and consider the way in which the non-finite clauses provide elaborating detail and information for the narrative.

Directly in front of them, **bordering** <u>the pavement</u>, there was a brick wall with fearsome-looking spikes all along the top of it.

He steered the trumpet through the curtains, far into the room, **aiming** <u>it at the place where he knew the bed to be</u>.

'I is going off **to wait** <u>in the garden</u>,' the BFG whispered.

Then there was a pause **punctuated** <u>by gasps</u> from the famous voice as the newspaper article was clearly being read and digested.

Non-finite clauses are useful because they are lexically dense — that is, they use fewer words to convey their meaning than the finite version. This is because the subject of the clause, the actor of the verb, is omitted from the clause and implied by the rest of the sentence. So, in the first example above, it is the wall that is the implied subject of the non-finite verb *bordering*: *A brick wall bordered the pavement*. Sometimes writers don't keep this consistency between the non-finite clause and the main clause, which has the subject, and can thus create sentences that are not entirely elegant or create ambiguity because the subject of the non-finite clause is not clear:

> *The girl with a dog **running** down the street*. Is it the girl or the dog that is the subject of *running*? So is it the girl and the dog running down the street, or is it just the dog?

> ***Dancing** faster and faster, the mother watched her daughter grow tired*. Is it the mother or the daughter who is the subject of dancing? So who is doing the dancing — the mother or the daughter?

Understanding clause punctuation

Developing children's understanding of clauses is a very helpful way to support deepening understanding of internal sentence punctuation.

Commas

We have already seen several ways in this chapter in which comma usage links to clauses, but let's pull it all together here, using examples from *The BFG*.

- Commas to replace *and* in a sequence of co-ordinated clauses:

  He took a deep breath, puffed out his cheeks and then whoof!

  He closed the lid, picked up the suitcase with one hand, took the pole with the net on the end in the other hand, and marched towards the entrance of the cave.

- Parenthetical commas around non-finite clauses and non-restrictive relative clauses to signal the information is additional and could be removed:

  Directly in front of them, bordering the pavement, there was a brick wall with fearsome-looking spikes all along the top of it.

  Sophie, who was also staring into the glass jar, cried out.

- Commas to demarcate a subordinate clause at the start of a sentence:

  When the BFG had consumed his seventy-second fried egg, Mr Tibbs sidled up to the Queen.

  Taking infinite care, the BFG unscrewed the top of the glass jar and tipped the squiggling squirming faintly scarlet trogglehumper into the wide end of his long trumpet.

  To manage this, the footmen had to stand on stepladders.

Colons and semi-colons

There is often disagreement about exactly when colons or semi-colons should be used, and a general tendency in modern texts to use far fewer than older texts used. However, they give writers more choices and possibilities about how to convey information within a sentence. A comma, semi-colon and colon are often described as being increasingly strong 'breaks' within a sentence, with the comma being a light break and a colon a distinct break. A more important distinction, though, is that a comma can never be substituted by a full stop, whereas a semi-colon and a colon are very often alternatives to using a full stop.

Semi-colons, like commas, are used to separate items in a list, and this can happen at the level of single words, phrases or clauses. The choice of whether to use a comma or a semi-colon is sometimes made because the semi-colons avoid ambiguity about what is being listed, but very often it is a writer's choice which to use. In the examples below, Eric Carle chooses to use a comma to separate the long list of noun phrases, describing the caterpillar's eating habits, whereas Kevin Crossley-Holland chooses semi-colons to separate the clauses in his story. You might think about whether there is any difference in the effect this has. Perhaps the comma creates more emphasis on the accumulation of foods the caterpillar has eaten and encourages an almost breathless pace of reading it? Perhaps the semi-colons make each clause more distinct, drawing attention to each individual activity that each child is undertaking for the woman?

How blessed that woman was. One girl pounded flour; another cut vegetables; another cooked; and another carried water from the well. One boy ploughed; one hunted; one fished; and one hauled some logs.

(*Short!*, Kevin Crossley-Holland)

On Saturday, he ate through one piece of chocolate cake, one ice-cream cone, one pickle, one slice of Swiss cheese, one slice of salami, one lollipop, one piece of cherry pie, one sausage, one cupcake, and one slice of watermelon.

(*The Very Hungry Caterpillar*, Eric Carle)

At clause level, semi-colons are used to link separate (independent) clauses that are closely related. It is another way of co-ordinating two or more clauses, and the semi-colon can substitute for 'and'. Again writers have their own preferred styles: Roald Dahl rarely uses any semi-colons, but A.A. Milne frequently uses them in *Winnie-the-Pooh*.

And as Piglet looked sorrowfully round, Eeyore picked the balloon up with his teeth, and placed it carefully in the pot; picked it out and put it on the ground; and then picked it up again and put it carefully back.

(*Winnie-the-Pooh*, A.A. Milne)

Colons are used to introduce or lead in to new information or ideas. They are often used to introduce a list, including a list of bullet points (as on a PowerPoint slide, for example), but they are also used in sentences to introduce a new idea that follows closely on from what has just been written. Whereas semi-colons are linking related ideas, and effectively co-ordinate information, a colon has a forward direction, leading the reader to expect new information. The clause before the colon must always be a main clause, but what comes after the colon can be a single word, a phrase, a clause or several clauses.

This was what Rabbit read out:

PLAN TO CAPTURE BABY ROO

(*Winnie-the-Pooh*, A.A. Milne)

He didn't reach up to Tom's knee and Tom thought he was the strangest thing he had ever set eyes on: brown and yellow all over, yellow and brown, with such a glint in his eye, and such a wizened face, that Tom felt afraid of him for all that he was so little and so old.

(Yallery Brown (in *Shorts!*), Kevin Crossley-Holland)

Dashes and brackets

Commas, dashes and brackets can all be used to create **parenthesis**, which is a section of a sentence that provides explanatory information, or a comment or aside. Parenthetical punctuation always comes in pairs of punctuation marks: a pair of commas, a pair of dashes or a pair of brackets. Parenthetical information can always be removed from the sentence without damaging the coherence, or sense, of the sentence. There are no rules about when you should use commas, dashes or brackets, and as with many aspects of internal sentence punctuation, it is a question of choosing the option that provides most clarity or matches the effect the writer desires. Commas are the most 'light touch' way of including parenthetical information. In general, brackets make the information less important or subsidiary to the general ideas in the sentence, whereas dashes seem to draw attention to the information in parenthesis. Too many brackets or too many dashes can be distracting, so they need to be used wisely. There is a lovely example in *Winnie-the-Pooh* where A.A. Milne uses all three techniques in one sentence, in a way that contributes to its humour.

And then this Bear, Pooh Bear, Winnie-the-Pooh, F.O.P (Friend of Piglet's), R.C. (Rabbit's Companion), P.D. (Pole Discoverer), E.C. and T.F. (Eeyore's Comforter and Tailfinder) — in fact, Pooh himself — said something so clever that Christopher Robin could only look at him with mouth open and eyes staring, wondering if this was really the Bear of Very Little Brain whom he had known and loved so long.

(*Winnie-the-Pooh*, A.A. Milne)

The dash can also be used to draw attention to an action or idea within the sentence without being parenthetical. The dash creates a visual break in the sentence, which can represent a break in the thoughts or speech of the writer or character, or which can simply draw our attention to that part of the sentence. Take a look at the examples below, taken from *The Very Hungry Caterpillar* and *Burglar Bill*, and consider why you think Eric Carle and the Ahlbergs chose to use dashes here.

One Sunday morning the warm sun came up and — pop! — out of the egg came a tiny and very hungry caterpillar.

Now he wasn't hungry any more — and he wasn't a caterpillar any more.

(*The Very Hungry Caterpillar*, Eric Carle)

That's a nice umbrella — I'll have that!

That's a nice tin of beans — I'll have that!

That's a nice date and walnut cake with buttercream filling and icing on the top — I'll have that!

(*Burglar Bill*, Janet and Allan Ahlberg)

Teaching activities

Problem pets: Writing a story using *Dear Zoo* as a model

Learning objective: To develop grammatical understanding of how clauses can be joined using simple co-ordinating conjunctions

Share together and enjoy the story *Dear Zoo* by Rod Campbell. This story uses the repeated structure of a sentence introducing the animal sent by the zoo and a following sentence explaining why the animal is a problem pet. For example, *They sent me a . . .* [picture of an elephant]. *He was too big.*

On a whiteboard, display all the introducing and explaining sentences in their matching pairs. For example:

They sent me a spider. He was too scary.

They sent me an elephant. He was too big.

Explain that Rod Campbell creates a three-sentence pattern in this story, which repeats several times through the book, using two sentences about the animal and a third sentence. Invite the children to suggest what the third sentence of this pattern is (*I sent him back!*), then explain that we could create a different pattern using *but* to join the first two sentences: *They sent me an elephant but he was too big. I sent him back!* Display this pattern on the whiteboard.

Ask children to write their own version of this story following the overall structure of the text as a model, but using this new pattern. They should think of different animals the zoo might send, and a different pet to end the story. If time allows, children could create their own *Dear Zoo* books, with text, illustrations and flaps.

When they have written their stories, invite one or two children to read their stories aloud, or ask them to read aloud to one another in pairs, so they can hear the patterns they have been creating. Then look again at the co-ordinated sentences, and draw out that we can join two sentences into one sentence using linking words (co-ordinating conjunctions) such as *and* or *but*.

Talk about it!

This activity provides several important opportunities for talk. The whiteboard activity introduces and develops understanding of simple sentences and how they can be joined into simple co-ordinated sentences; the writing of the story using the model offers the opportunity for one-to-one discussion with children as they write, to embed the ability to write co-ordinated sentences; and the closing discussion allows you to secure and consolidate their understanding, and to introduce the grammatical terminology if appropriate.

- During the whiteboard activity, ask questions that develop understanding of the sentence and how it can be joined, encouraging them to imitate the model sentences. This might include questions such as:
  - » What is the verb? How do you know?
  - » Can you create another sentence like this about an animal the zoo might send as a pet?
  - » These are two short sentences — can you join them to make one longer sentence?

Invite children to read aloud the three-sentence pattern in the original and their new two-sentence patterns, exploring how they can be read differently with different expression.

- During the writing activity, move round the classroom looking at children's emerging texts, and ask individuals questions that invite them to explain what they have done or that help them to clarify any misunderstandings you may see.
- During the closing discussion, ask questions that pin down their understanding of how *but* can join two sentences as in their texts, and extend this to an understanding of how *and* can also join sentences. This might include questions such as:
  - » Which word have you used to make the sentences join?
  - » Are there other conjunctions you could use to join sentences like this?
  - » Could you join your second sentence to your first sentence to make an even longer sentence (e.g. *They sent me an elephant but he was too big so I sent him back!*)?
  - » Which pattern do you prefer and why?

Notes for teachers

1. There is a video of *Dear Zoo* you might like to use: www.youtube.com/watch?v=Kzl9IyeMWto

2. The primary purpose of this activity is to develop understanding of how to join two simple sentences, but it gives you an opportunity to teach the word *conjunction* as explicit grammatical terminology.

3. The repeated patterns of clauses in this book also give you a chance to consolidate other grammatical terminology if the children have already started to learn them, particularly the nouns for the animals and the adjectives used to describe the animals.

4. Through the lesson, they will encounter the original three-sentence version, write their own two-sentence version and, in the final discussion, explore the possibility of a one-sentence version. Encourage them to see these all as possibilities from which they can choose, rather than suggesting any one version is better than the others.

Be the expert: Exploring subordinate clauses in information texts

Learning objective: To develop grammatical understanding of how subordinate clauses are important in information texts to provide explanatory detail

Share the reading of an information text, such as the Eyewitness Guide, *Ancient Egypt*, which is relevant to a topic you are studying. Find a section of the text where the writer uses subordinate clauses as part of the explanation. Prepare a worksheet with the subordinate clauses removed from the text, and reproduced at the bottom, as in the example below, taken from *Ancient Egypt*. Ask the children to work in pairs and decide which subordinate clauses should go in which box in the text.

_____, its walls would be covered with plaster, and the inside was often painted — either with patterns or scenes from nature. Inside, the houses were cool, _____

_____. Wealthy families had large houses. Beyond the hall would be bedrooms and private apartments, and stairs to the roof. The kitchen was some distance from the living rooms, _____

_____. The Egyptians held parties in their homes _____

_____.

to keep smells away

when a house was built

which the children enjoyed as much as their parents

as the small windows let in only a little light

As a class, discuss the answers to this activity, exploring any occasions where a pair have put a subordinate clause in an inappropriate sentence. Draw out how these clauses are explanatory, providing additional or essential information to the reader about life in an Egyptian house.

Talk about it!

There are two principal opportunities to exploit the power of talk in this activity. First, the paired task, matching the subordinate clause to its sentence, generates peer-to-peer talk in which they will have to explain to each other their reasoning about where to place the clause, and through this show their understanding of coherence in a sentence. Second, the whole-class task is the key point at which their understanding of how the subordinate clauses provide explanatory information is developed.

- During the paired task, build on their peer talk by probing their decision-making about the coherence of the text. This might include questions such as:
  » What made you put that subordinate clause in that sentence?
  » Which words give you clues that this subordinate clause belongs in this sentence?
  » Why can't I put this subordinate clause here [moving a clause to an inappropriate place]?
  » Why do you think it is a subordinate clause?
- During the whole-class plenary activity, use the discussion to ensure all children have understood the purpose of these subordinate clauses in this text, focusing on the explanatory detail they provide. This might include question such as:
  » What information does this subordinate clause give us about Egyptian homes?
  » Which of these subordinate clauses could be left out of the text completely (although we would lose information)?
  » Could you rewrite any of these sentences in a different way, conveying the same information but not using these subordinate clauses?

Notes for teachers

1. The four clauses include two finite subordinate clauses (*when . . . ; as . . .*), a relative clause (*which . . .*) and a non-finite clause (*to . . .*). Children may not need to know this detail, but it is good for you to be clear about the three different types of subordinate clause here.

2. Three of the clauses in this passage can be removed completely without damaging the sense of the sentences, but the first example, *When a house was built,* cannot be left out because the rest of the sentence needs it to make sense. So here you can see that three of the clauses provide *additional* explanatory information, whereas the *when* clause provides *essential* explanatory information.

3. Avoid spending too much time in the plenary on determining where the clauses go in the text. Deal with this quickly, so that maximum time is available for the discussion about how the subordinate clauses provide explanatory information.

4. You could follow up this task by asking children to write a paragraph of an information text, and then to annotate their texts with comments on how they have used them. This kind of activity helps to draw out explicit understanding.

Games box

In advance, prepare a set of large floor cards with a range of co-ordinating and subordinating conjunctions on them, including some repetitions of common ones. Also prepare a Story Starter bag, containing artefacts that can trigger a plot line (such as a letter, a lock of hair, a mirror, a set of keys, etc.).

Create a circle as a whole class and put the floor cards in a pile face down in the centre of the circle. Invite one child to take one artefact out of the Story Starter bag. Give everyone one minute to think about possible story lines this artefact suggests. Then ask the child with the artefact to begin the story by telling the first clause only of the story; the child next to her picks up one of the conjunction cards and adds a new clause to the story using that conjunction. Any child can end a sentence by saying 'full stop' and then starting a new sentence. Prepare for some bizarre stories!

Tackling misconceptions

1. Many primary teachers use an acronym, FANBOYS, to introduce children to co-ordinating conjunctions. The acronym stands for: For, And, Nor, But, Or, Yet and So.

    This is a very unhelpful and confusing acronym because, in modern English, *for* and *yet* are very rarely used as conjunctions, and are much more commonly used as a preposition or an adverb.

    > I took my umbrella **for** I feared it would rain. (conjunction)
    >
    > I ran **for** my life. (preposition)
    >
    > I knew it was wrong **yet** I still stole the apple. (conjunction)
    >
    > I haven't had my dinner **yet**. (adverb)

    Similarly, while *nor* is a conjunction it needs its partner, *neither*, to be coherent.

    > He had **neither** money, **nor** a job. (conjunction linking two nouns)
    >
    > He **neither** walks to school **nor** does his homework. (conjunction linking two clauses)

2. Co-ordinated clauses form compound sentences, but this is often taught as though a compound sentence can only have two clauses joined by *and, but, or* or *so*. In fact, as we have seen in the examples in this chapter, a sentence can have any number of co-ordinated clauses. With young children, introduce them to simple co-ordination

that does link two clauses, but make sure you also show them simple examples of more than two co-ordinated clauses in a sentence. The *Three Little Pigs* example of *He huffed and he puffed and he blew the house down* is a good example, as so many children are familiar with it already. With older children, introduce them to sentence examples that use commas as well as *and/but/or/so* to link co-ordinated clauses.

3.   Older children, and indeed many adults, make the mistake of using *however* as a conjunction joining clauses in the middle of a sentence, when it is actually an adverb (like *moreover, on the other hand, similarly*). Either a new sentence is needed, beginning with *however*, or a semi-colon can be used:

Fox-hunting is cruel, however, it should not be banned. ✗

Fox-hunting is cruel; however, it should not be banned. ✓

Fox-hunting is cruel. However, it should not be banned. ✓

6
Sentences

What you need to know

The sentence is the vital unit of meaning in writing, but it's actually quite difficult to explain what a sentence is. Look at what these children have to say about the sentence and decide how helpful their definitions are. What do they seem to have understood and what do they seem confused about?

- A sentence is about ten words that end in a full stop.
- It's when you stop talking about one thing and start talking about something else, or when you take a breath or something.
- It's got to have a doing word and it's got to make sense.
- You don't normally start a sentence with 'And' — we got taught you shouldn't do it.

A common definition of a sentence is that it starts with a capital letter, ends with a full stop, has a subject and a verb, and makes complete sense, but the trouble with teaching this as a 'golden rule' for sentences is that lots of everyday examples of writing don't fit it. You only have to think of newspaper headlines, book titles, advertising slogans or signs (e.g. *Royal Baby Fever, No ball games, Disneyland — the happiest place on Earth*) to see that they 'make complete sense' without using any terminal punctuation and often consist only of noun phrases. And what about the three examples below? Very many of the stories and poems you share in class will 'break the rules' in the sense that their sentence patterns don't fit the standard definition.

Uh-uh! Mud!

Thick oozy mud.

We can't go over it.

We can't go under it.

Oh no!

(*We're Going on a Bear Hunt*, Michael Rosen)

OKAY, OKAY. So hang me. I killed the bird. For pity's sake, I'm a cat.

(*The Diary of a Killer Cat*, Anne Fine)

I looked but I could see nothing at first. But then as I looked I saw the surface of the lake shiver and break. And, to my amazement, up out of the lake came a shining sword, a hand holding it, and an arm in a white silk sleeve.

(*Arthur, High King of Britain*, Michael Morpurgo)

In the light of these examples, how might *you* explain what a sentence is?

You might have said that single words and interjections can be sentences, that sentences don't always have a subject or verb, and can indeed start with a co-ordinating conjunction as a stylistic choice. In fact, many texts deliberately play with syntactic rules to achieve a particular effect — for example, to mirror the lively rhythms and patterns of everyday speech, or to foreground particular words or ideas. And how are sentences shaped in poetry? Because the 'rules' for end-of-line or mid-line punctuation are so flexible, poetry offers tremendous scope for trying out and evaluating different syntactic effects.

Many of the sentences in the examples above happen to be short, but of course there are no fixed rules about sentence length. A lovely example of a sentence being pushed to its limits is this one from Philip Pullman's description of the bear fight in *Northern Lights*. The main clause and its finite verb have been highlighted for you. As you read, count the number of subordinate clauses that go before and after this main clause. Then consider the effect of this very long multi-clause sentence: what impression of the bear fight does Pullman want to create?

Like a wave that has been building its strength over a thousand miles of ocean, and which makes little stir in the deep water, but which when it reaches the shallows rears itself up high into the sky, terrifying the shore-dwellers, before crashing down on the land with irresistible power — so Iorek Byrnison **rose up against Iofur**, exploding upwards from his firm footing on the dry rock and slashing with a ferocious left hand at the exposed jaw of Iofur Raknison.

You could say that the gradual build-up of successive clauses heightens the drama of the fight between the bears, with the tension ratcheted up until the vicious blow is delivered; the complex structure of the sentence mirrors the epic nature of the clash between these two enemies. Of course, there is a subjectivity to this kind of explanation of effects, but we have found that children often struggle to explain the impact on the reader of grammatical choices, so that it's helpful for you to model this for them, using language that's accessible for the age group and over time building children's vocabulary for explaining and evaluating effects.

We have also found that, if children are taught rigid definitions or rules about the sentence, they are likely to be puzzled by examples that don't conform to expectations, and they may be less likely to take risks and experiment with sentence variation in their own writing. Teaching about sentences, then, can usefully emphasise how flexible the sentence is as a unit of meaning, and focus on building children's understanding of the choices available to them that will achieve specific effects in specific writing contexts. This chapter outlines the grammatical knowledge that will support your confidence in doing so.

Understanding the sentence

David Crystal points out that 'a sentence is the chief means we have of organising our thoughts so that they make sense, both to ourselves and to others' (1996: 21). To make sense, a sentence needs to:

- **be grammatical** — words within a sentence are grammatically connected and sequenced, so that *Sunday Grandma visited on we* is clearly not a sentence, whereas *We visited Grandma on Sunday* does make grammatical sense and is the most likely sequence.
- **be complete** — one or more words that can be understood readily in their context, e.g. *We visited on.* is clearly incomplete in any context and needs finishing.

Unless they are learning English as a second language, children are unlikely to make fundamental grammatical mistakes with word order in sentences. 'Ungrammatical sentences' are more likely to be related to non-Standard English dialects or the differences between speech and writing. (For more about this, see Chapter 8.) A more common difficulty for children is knowing when a sentence is 'finished', and therefore where to place boundary punctuation. Clearly, the idea that you start a new sentence 'when you take a breath' is both insufficient and misleading, worryingly dependent on lung capacity! Understanding the rules that govern the construction of sentences — the syntactic possibilities and probabilities — will help children make sense of what they are reading, and help them shape and control their writing.

Syntactic structure: clause elements

To remind you, a sentence can consist of just one clause (a simple sentence with one finite verb) or a number of clauses that are linked through co-ordination or subordination. Each *clause* in a sentence is made up of different combinations of the following elements: the subject (S), the verb (V), the object (O), the complement (C) and the adverbial (A).

- The **subject** tells us the theme of the sentence, who or what is the actor of the verb. The subject is usually a single noun, a noun phrase or a pronoun.

- The (finite) **verb** is the most important element because it makes a sentence complete.

- The **object** identifies who or what is on the receiving end of the verb. The object is a single noun, a noun phrase or a pronoun.

- The **complement** is the term used for one or more words that come after particular verbs, called linking verbs, to complete the meaning of either a subject or object. If you can't remove it from the sentence, then it's likely to be a complement, as here: *He was famished; Oak trees can be very tall*. Linking verbs are most often a form of *be* (*is*, *was*, etc.); other examples include a*ppear, turn, feel, seem, grow*. Complements are often adjectives or noun phrases.

- The **adverbial** tells us more about how, when or where something happened. Adverbials can be a single adverb, an adverbial phrase or a subordinate clause.

As you read the examples of single-clause sentences below, from *The Iron Man*, by Ted Hughes, explain to yourself how each element is working within the sentence — what its purpose or function is. You can clarify this by mentally removing each element and seeing what happens to the meaning of the sentence. As a further check on understanding, see if you can substitute each element with another choice that would make sense.

S V A

The Iron Man/came/to the top of the cliff.

S V O

He/was hearing/the sea.

S V C

He/felt/afraid.

S V A

The wind/sang/through his iron fingers.

Each element can consist of one word or more than one word. Why is it important for children to know this? (See 'Tackling misconceptions' at the end of this chapter for comments.)

It is our understanding of syntactic possibilities and probabilities that can help us notice unusual sentence patterns. Look again at this sentence from Michael Morpurgo's *Arthur, High King of Britain*:

And, to my amazement, up out of the lake came a shining sword, a hand holding it, and an arm in a white silk sleeve.

The order of elements in most statement sentences is subject + verb (SV) so that we might expect this:

S V

. . . a shining sword/came/up out of the lake . . .

Instead, the subject of the sentence is placed *after* the finite verb:

V S

. . . up out of the lake/came/a shining sword . . .

The sentence is also notable because both the subject and the finite verb come late in the sentence, after the adverbial element (the underlined prepositional phrases):

And, <u>to my amazement</u>, <u>up out of the lake</u> came a shining sword . . .

Subject–verb inversions like this always delay the revealing of the subject. But the purpose or effect of this delay is different according to the context in which it appears. Here you might describe the subject–verb inversion as building up the drama, delaying the moment when the magical sword, Excalibur, appears! Or you might feel it represents grammatically the visual effect of the sword rising out of the water. In other contexts, the subject–verb inversion might create suspense or surprise, or alternatively may allow the writer to foreground different information at the beginning of the sentence. Manipulating syntactic structure, therefore, is an important way of achieving sentence variety.

Understanding sentence types

All sentences can be grouped into two main categories, as described below.

Minor sentences (or irregular sentences)

These do not follow all the syntactic rules. They are particularly common in signs and labels, titles and sub-headings, sayings and idioms, everyday conversations and dialogue in fiction. They are also common in many of the texts children read, and are a very common stylistic feature of effective writing. Look at this example from *Don't Forget Tiggs* by Michael Rosen:

And then, Mr Hurry. Off he hurried. Out of the house, down the road, off to work. Whoosh!

Only one of the sentences, the second, is a complete sentence. The other three are all minor sentences without a finite verb. The verbless sentences refer back to what's already been said, and the interjection *Whoosh!* makes perfect sense as a representation of Mr Hurry's hurriedness!

Major sentences (or regular sentences)

These are the most common type, and typical of more formal writing. They *always* contain a finite verb, usually contain a subject and may contain other clause elements such as an adverbial.

- *Hurry!* (implied second-person subject + finite verb)
- *They hurried.* (pronoun subject + finite verb)
- *The children hurried down the road.* (noun phrase subject + finite verb + adverbial)

You will see from this that the finite verb is the vital component in a major sentence and it's worth spending time to secure children's understanding of this. You may want to look back to the section on finite verbs in Chapter 2 at this point to check your own understanding of their function.

Sentences are also classified according to the function they perform, and there are four different types, each with distinctive grammatical patterns. Using the examples from the table, what can you say about the **subject** and the <u>finite verb</u> in each example?

Sentence type	Example	Function
Statement	**The Iron Man** <u>came</u> to the top of the cliff.	Conveys information
Question	How far <u>had</u> **he** walked?	Seeks answers
Command	<u>Hush</u>.	Gives an instruction
Exclamation	**An Iron Man! A giant!**	Expresses strong emotion

A **statement** (or declarative sentence) is the most common type. Typically, the subject comes before the verb and is often placed at the beginning of a sentence, a 'normal' pattern that helps us to spot variations like this one: *Never before <u>had</u> **the Iron Man** <u>seen</u> the sea.*

A **question** (or interrogative sentence) can start with a question word (*who, what, why, how,* etc.) or an auxiliary verb (*are, do, have,* etc.). A question can also end with a question tag that invites confirmation: *You saw the Iron Man, didn't you?* A rhetorical question is structured as a question but doesn't require an answer: *Who can say where the Iron Man came from?*

A **command** (or imperative sentence) has an implied subject (*you*) and a verb in the imperative mood. It may start with *Do* for emphasis or to sound polite (*Do come inside*) or *Don't* to create a negative (*Don't leave the house*). In some forms a command has a stated subject: *Let <u>me</u> finish*; <u>Everybody</u>, *listen up!* <u>Matilda</u>, *be quiet.* Imperatives are always in the present tense.

An **exclamation** is a sentence that expresses strong emotion, such as surprise, pleasure, humour or anger. The exclamation mark suggests the necessary tone of voice and emphasis: *How dreadful! You must be joking!* Because they are associated with informal, conversational texts, exclamations are often minor sentences or interjections: *A giant! Crash!*

Different kinds of texts often have characteristic sentence types that children will need to be able to imitate in order to 'sound like an expert' in that text type: instructional texts have a high proportion of commands; information texts rely more on statements. A writing task might usefully be supported by collecting examples from the target text type to use as models.

Understanding sentence variety

Confident writers deliberately vary the sentence types and structures they use, and because sentence variety is a key marker for progression in writing, it often features in class or individual targets. However, we have found that children's understanding of the term, and of how to achieve it, can be quite limited: top picks from children for how to improve writing are adding more adjectives and adverbs and using lots of 'short snappy sentences'! Of course there is no intrinsic merit in using a short sentence or in starting a sentence with an adverb, so that it's helpful to frame such features as *possible* choices, dependent on writing purpose and intended effect, and some suggested effects are included in the information that follows.

As well as the choice of statements, questions, commands and exclamations, writers can choose from the following.

Different sentence lengths

Short sentences can be effective for:

- making key points in an argument — for example, at the start or end of a paragraph: *Wild animals should not be kept in zoos . . . In conclusion, zoos are cruel and unnatural.*
- stating a topic sentence in an information text: *Animals build many types of homes.*
- creating a quick pace in a narrative or emphasising key ideas, as Ted Hughes does here: *Hogarth began to run. He ran and ran. Home. Home. The Iron Man had come back.*

Longer sentences can be effective for adding descriptive or explanatory detail, to make a scene easier to visualise or an idea easier to understand:

Here and there lay half a wheel, or half an axle, or half a mudguard, carved with giant toothmarks where it had been bitten off.

(*The Iron Man*, Ted Hughes)

You might also consider the rhythmic patterns created when writers deliberately contrast long and short sentences. For example, in his description of the bear fight in *Northern Lights*, quoted earlier in this chapter, Philip Pullman follows an 82-word sentence with this: *It was a horrifying blow.*

Different clause structures

As described in Chapter 5, sentences can consist of a single clause or multiple clauses. A simple sentence has one clause containing a finite verb; and multi-clause sentences have two or more finite clauses, held together by co-ordination or a combination of finite and subordinate clauses. Below are three sentences from *The Iron Man* that exemplify these three patterns:

- *His iron ears <u>turned</u>, this way, that way.* (simple sentence)
- *At last he <u>stopped</u>, and <u>looked</u> at the sea.* (compound sentence)
- *He <u>swayed</u> in the strong wind <u>that pressed against his back</u>.* (complex sentence)

Children may have picked up the idea that achieving variety in sentence structures is an aim in itself, which seems to underlie this comment from a child we interviewed: 'I need to vary my sentence variety: she's said that a lot in the marking she does.' It's important that you help children to tie choices of sentence structure to a purpose and effect, bearing in mind the type of text being written. For example, a single-clause sentence (which can be any length) can be effective for:

- focusing attention on a single idea or argument:
  Endangered animals like the tiger or the panda <u>need</u> *the protection of zoos.*
- drawing attention to an expressive choice of verb:
  A few rocks <u>tumbled</u> *with him.*

Co-ordinated clauses can be effective for:

- chaining ideas, often to create pace:
  It ran forward suddenly, grabbed something and tugged.
- balancing ideas and providing contrast:
  Some animals build nests, but others make dens or dig burrows.

Subordinate clauses can be effective for:

- adding layers of detail:
  Finally, the footprints led back up to the top of the cliff, <u>where the little boy had seen the Iron Man appear the night before, when he was fishing</u>.
- stressing the relationship between ideas:
  <u>*Although zoos are unnatural*</u>, *they do protect endangered species.*

Thematic variety: different ways of starting a sentence

As we have seen, the most common sentence pattern is to write the subject first, followed by the verb, but if this is over-done it can lead to a very repetitive rhythm to the text. You can see this in the example from a child's narrative below — the repeated subject start creates an almost clipped rhythm, and also reduces the connecting of ideas between sentences. You could move several of the sentences to different positions, and it would make little difference.

We were off to the beach called Sunny Cove. **The wind** was blowing in our faces. **We** are finally there. **I** set up the tent and looked around. **I** was a bit scared but it was quite fun.

There are many ways to create thematic variety by starting a sentence in a different way, but the most common are probably:

- adverbs — *quickly, first, unfortunately, next*, etc.
- adverbial phrases of time — *later that day, that evening*, etc.
- prepositional phrases — *in the garden, below the stairs, with regret*, etc.
- finite subordinate clauses — *when I had eaten my dinner, after they left*, etc.
- non-finite subordinate clauses — *standing silently, struck by fear*, etc.

In terms of the syntactic elements of a clause discussed earlier, all of these grammatical structures tend to perform the adverbial function in a clause, but if you are teaching about thematic variety it is helpful to consider this range of grammatical possibilities for starting a sentence.

Have a look at the thematic variety in the extract below. Can you name the different grammatical structures used to begin the sentences, and can you hear the different textual rhythm it creates?

> <u>When the farmers realized that the Iron Man had freed himself</u> they groaned. What could they do now? They decided to call the Army, who could pound him to bits with anti-tank guns. But Hogarth had another idea. <u>At first</u>, the farmers would not hear of it, least of all his own father . . . <u>After spending a night</u> and a day eating all the barbed wire for miles around, as well as hinges he tore off gates and the tin cans he found in ditches, and three new tractors and two cars and a lorry, the Iron Man was resting in a clump of elm trees. <u>There</u> he stood, leaning among the huge branches, almost hidden by the dense leaves, his eyes glowing a soft blue.

Sentence punctuation

Chapter 5 focused on internal sentence punctuation. Boundary punctuation refers to choices that mark the end of one complete unit of sense, whether this is a single word or a number of clauses. The choices are: full stop, question mark, exclamation mark and ellipsis, which can be used to indicate an exaggerated pause, as here:

> Sometimes, in the rain and dark, worms come up from underground. They seem too small to be important, but watch . . . the worms are recycling.
>
> (*A First Book of Nature*, Nicola Davies)

Bullet points can also function as boundary punctuation, for example by separating complete steps in a process or set of instructions, introduced with a colon or organised under a heading, as in this example.

> ### Worms: Why They Are Slimy and Other Facts
>
> * A worm has no eyes, legs or arms.
> * There can be up to one MILLION earthworms in just one acre of land.
> * The sticky slime a worm makes helps keep it from drying out. If the worm dries out, it will die, because it breathes through its skin.
>
> (www.worm-farming.com)

A comma is *never* used as boundary punctuation, although using a comma instead of a full stop is a very common mistake, for adults as well as children. What do you think might cause confusion here, and how might you tackle this in the classroom?

Teaching activities

Long and short: Writing the climax to the story of Daedalus and Icarus

Learning objective: Understand how to vary sentence length to create interest and drama for the reader

Share the story of Daedalus and Icarus by telling it yourself, or by listening to or reading a favourite version. You can also show Pieter Brueghel's painting, 'The Fall of Icarus', to support understanding of the story and as a prompt for gathering vocabulary for the writing task. Using a story mountain if helpful, clarify the shape of the story and explain that they will be writing the climax to it, where Icarus soars too close to the sun, melting the wax on his wings and plunging into the sea. Share initial ideas about how they can make this part of the story the most exciting part.

On a whiteboard, show a 'first draft' that consists of a series of short one-clause sentences with repetitive S + V and S + V + O patterns, reading aloud so children can hear the monotonous rhythm:

> Icarus flew higher and higher. He flew towards the sun. He looked down at the sea. Icarus felt very small. He was afraid. He couldn't see his father any more. He started to fall. He knew he would die.

Explain the focus on varying the length of sentences, which includes using *some* short sentences to heighten the drama. You can ask which *two* of these short sentences they think are the most dramatic — they can save these to use in their own version. Model how to create sentences of different lengths, generating as many examples as you think helpful:

> Icarus flew higher and higher.
>
> Icarus flew higher and higher towards the sun.
>
> Icarus flew higher and higher until he felt he was almost touching the sun.
>
> Whooping loudly, Icarus flew higher and higher, soaring towards the sun like a bird.

Keep the examples displayed as children write their own version of the episode, aiming for deliberate variation in sentence lengths. You can provide a pattern for them to follow if you like, such as 1 short + 1 medium + 1 long + 1 short. Encourage them to try several versions and to read aloud to one another to hear the rhythms they are creating. Ask them to explain which short sentences they have used from the draft version, where they have placed them, and why.

Talk about it!

This activity provides opportunities for several different kinds of talk. If you are using a printed version of the story, you can ask pairs to investigate sentence length specifically, and to report examples of the shortest and longest sentences they have found. The whiteboard modelling activity allows for explicit whole-class discussion of how short sentences can be expanded and joined in different ways, with grammatical terminology used as appropriate. Children can create their own version of the story climax independently or collaboratively; reading aloud to one another encourages them to hear the sentence rhythms created, and explaining where they have positioned the very short sentences encourages explanation of intended effects.

- During the whiteboard activity, ask questions that develop understanding of the sentence, and how it can be expanded and joined, encouraging them to imitate the models by writing different-length versions of one of the other short sentences. Check understanding through questions such as:
    » What is the finite verb? How do you know? Can you choose a better finite verb?
    » Which subordinating conjunctions could we use to join sentences?
    » Can you create another prepositional phrase that tells us where Icarus was flying?
    » Can you create another subordinate clause that tells us how Icarus was flying?
    » How can we make this sentence even longer? Is it now too long?
- Support children's discussion of choices and their effects by providing prompt questions such as:
    » Which sentence sounds fast when you read it? Which one sounds slower?
    » Which sentence do you most like the sound of?
    » Which sentence makes you feel frightened for Icarus?
    » Which sentence sounds the most exciting?
    » Why did you choose that sentence to end with?
    » What did you want your reader to think or feel when they read that sentence?

Notes for teachers

1. You could watch a version of the story or share together a printed version; there are lots of versions to choose from on the internet, many of which will have good examples of shorter and longer sentences that you can use as models.
2. In terms of achieving sentence variety, the focus here is on varying the length of sentences, which is accessible for many children, but this can be altered to suit your class's needs. For example, you could focus on:
    » using a wider range of lexical finite verbs in co-ordinated sentences: *Icarus tumbled out of the sky and plunged towards the sea.*
    » non-finite subordinate clauses in different positions within the sentence, to emphasise the speed with which Icarus falls: *Tumbling and twisting, Icarus fell, swooping towards the waves, plunging like a stone into the sea.*

> » the effects of positioning the subject after the verb, a feature of older stories, to create the style of a myth: *In his glistening white feathers, up and up, far too close to the sun flew Icarus.*

Try always to be specific about the effect you are trying to achieve, and encourage children to do the same, in their own words.

3. The emphasis here is on varying sentence length by adding clauses and adverbial detail, rather than noun phrase detail. This is to encourage children to move beyond 'adding adjectives' to make a sentence longer. You can also use this activity to consolidate understanding of finite and non-finite verbs and their function.

Classroom rules: Write a poem using 'Don't Lean Back on Your Chair, Claire', by Jez Alborough, as a model

Learning objective: To secure understanding of grammatical patterns used in commands

---

Prepare a set of cards for each table group showing typical classroom commands (including your own favourites). For example, *Stop talking and look this way. Put your pens down now! Take your coats off. Go outside and play.* Ask children to practise reading them aloud, one by one or as a whole group, thinking about the tone of voice that is needed, then count down to a whole-class 'performance'.

Read and enjoy the poem 'Don't Lean Back on Your Chair, Claire', by Jez Alborough. Show the poem and explore its patterns, highlighting how the commands are varied from verse to verse.

Ask children to contribute more examples of 'classroom rules' — what else have they heard teachers say they should and shouldn't do? List a selection on the whiteboard or on blank cards provided for each table group. Use examples from them to model the composition of an additional verse for the poem, using a different child's name. You can concentrate on the rhythm of each line to prevent rhyme becoming a distraction, and choose a simpler couplet format, for example:

> Don't ask to stay in at break, Jack/Get out in the fresh air instead.

> Sit on the carpet nicely, Louise/Stop wriggling about like a worm.

Leaving the model displayed, ask children to compose their own verse, using their own name, or an invented one if they prefer. There is no need to make the lines rhyme; concentrate on line length and rhythm instead. Share examples of children's new lines, reading them alongside the original.

End by sharing another poem on the theme of classroom rules: 'Scissors', by Allan Ahlberg (www.poetryarchive.org/poem/scissors).

Talk about it!

You can use a choral reading of the poem to help draw attention to its patterns: you could ask children to join in on the refrain in the final line of each verse, or to emphasise the different commands. Encourage them to re-read lines frequently as they compose, to adjust the rhythms so that their lines 'match' the original. Ask them to learn the lines they compose, so they can insert them into the original as fluently as possible.

Notes for teachers

1. You can vary the examples you provide on cards, to include negative commands (*Don't run in the corridor!*) and more polite commands (*Please stop talking; Do take care on the stairs*). Use this as a chance to recap or clarify typical features of commands: short sentences consisting of finite verbs without a subject, with the verb at the start or close to the start, ending in either a full stop or exclamation mark.

2. 'Don't Lean Back on Your Chair, Claire' can be found in Jez Alborough's *Guess What Happened at School Today*, published by HarperCollins Children's Books (2003).

3. When you explore the poem, ensure that children can see the finite verbs in each verse: *lean, use, sit, stop, pick up, bring, take.* For extra support, you can use these verbs in a simpler composing task, asking children to substitute alternatives — for example, *Don't lean back on your chair, Claire* could be changed to *Don't lean your head on the table, Sam; Stop rocking about in the air, Claire* could be changed to *Stop tapping your ruler on the table, Ruth.*

4. For extra challenge, explore the use of exclamation marks and ellipsis in the original poem, explaining how they add to the humour. Can children use similar effects in their own verses?

Games box

Replacing punctuation: Give pairs a sentence from a story, a verse from a poem or a short extract of dialogue, with the punctuation blanked out and listed below the extract. Ask them to put the punctuation back in so that the text makes sense and shows us how to read it. An extract like this from *The Rascally Cake* by Jeanne Willis would be a good choice:

'Whoops!' exclaimed Rufus, 'I've made a mistake,

Something's gone terribly wrong with this cake.

I've used too much flour . . . the fat was too hot.'

Off flew the dustbin lid! Out the cake got!

Get them to compare their version with the original and explain any differences (more than one version will be feasible).

Repeat the pattern: Write up a sentence that follows a pattern you want children to learn, either because it's important to a particular text type or because it's important for their progress as writers — for example, adding descriptive detail or information about people, using a relative clause starting with '*who*' and parenthetical commas:

Holly, who forgot to set her alarm clock, was late for school.

Ask children to repeat the pattern, changing the name and the relative clause:

Ben, who missed the bus, was late for school.

The teacher, who thought it was Sunday, was late for school.

Generate examples together, then ask children to create and share their own, using mini-whiteboards. You can score/deduct points for accurate/inaccurate punctuation.

Tongue-twisting sentences: This is a game to reinforce understanding of word-class choices and their sequence in a single-clause sentence. Prepare cards with a simple noun phrase on one side and a single verb or verb phrase on the other. An alphabetical animal theme would work well and you can use alliteration to make it fun and to focus children's choices — for example, bumble bees/are buzzing; a cat/crouches; an elephant/enjoys; four fish/flash by. Using mini-whiteboards, ask pairs to write a simple sentence using only the noun and verb, punctuated correctly. Model how to expand a sentence, following a specific instruction, asking children to try this out on their own sentence each time.

- Describe your animal with an adjective: *A cowardly cat crouches.*
- Use a prepositional phrase to say where your animal is: *A cowardly cat crouches in a corner.*
- Use an adverb to say more about how your animal moves: *A cowardly cat crouches carefully in a corner.*

Ask children to rearrange the words to create the best tongue-twister they can while still making sense: *Carefully in a corner crouches a cowardly cat.* Then ask children to say the tongue-twisters, repeating them as quickly and as accurately as they can.

Tackling misconceptions

1. Identifying the subject and the verb in a sentence

The term 'subject' is a difficult one for children to understand grammatically; they are more likely to think of it literally, as a topic or a school subject. Some children have learned that a subject is a single noun, but the subject might be an expanded noun phrase or it might be a pronoun. Showing children that clause elements can be one word or a phrase will help them see the range of possible choices, for example between a single adverb and a prepositional phrase, as well as highlighting which elements have fixed positions and which can be moved around. It might also help children see how to make changes to a 'grammatical chunk' of the sentence in order to improve it, rather than adding or substituting single words, which isn't always effective.

2. Boundary punctuation

The idea that you put a full stop 'where you take a breath' is not at all helpful. Children who have been taught this will often say that a comma marks 'a small breath' and a full stop 'a big breath', which does not help them see the grammatical function of these punctuation marks. Additionally, children often talk about 'adding in punctuation' when they have finished writing, rather than seeing it as essential to meaning-making during composition. They also talk of 'adding more' punctuation without links being made to grammatical function: the idea that adding more exclamation marks will automatically make writing 'more exciting' is surprisingly common! It's essential therefore to reinforce use of boundary punctuation at the point of writing, linked firmly to the sentence types the text demands, rather than seeing it as something to be tackled at the proofreading stage.

7
Vocabulary

Many of the activities in this book have focused on noticing the grammatical choices made by 'real writers' to support young writers in exercising choice in their own writing. This act of choosing and evaluating is partially dependent on the breadth of vocabulary a child can draw on. This chapter looks at ways teachers might develop and extend a child's vocabulary. This focus on words, word families and word patterns, and how they can communicate more than literal meaning, aims to develop sophistication in word choice, but might also support spelling, through drawing attention to common patterns, roots and form. It is informed by two of the principles that capture our approach to teaching writing with grammar, namely (1) the use of activities that support children in making choices, and (2) encouraging playful experimentation with language. The main content of the chapter is a varied collection of classroom-based activities and ideas. We hope you will be able to take them, adapt them and build them in to existing schemes of work. For every activity, there will also be a commentary on why and how the understanding they capture might support writing in particular and knowledge about language more broadly. The activities are organised around three themes: the subtlety that word choice can offer a writer; how playing with different grammatical forms can offer a choice beyond the lexical meaning; and finally how knowing these things can enable us to be creative and playful with the English language.

Words can capture subtle differences

In his book, *Mother Tongue*, Bill Bryson (2009) comments that 'the richness of the English vocabulary and the wealth of available synonyms means that English speakers can often draw shades of distinctions unavailable to non-English speakers'. In classrooms this potential richness is often facilitated by the use of a thesaurus. Of course the danger of this is that, while there may be many words with similar meanings, casually replacing one word with another is rarely a good strategy and so while a thesaurus can offer alternatives, it does not support the judgement required to decide which word to use. Indeed children might simply select the most exotic or unfamiliar word, believing 'unusual' is best. This may be reinforced by the way we, as teachers, privilege some words over others, describing them as 'wow' powers or powerful words, as if the word itself has some innate value, separate from the context in which it was written. Clearly there are times when the simple 'cat-like' is more appropriate than the sophistication of 'feline', or when the slightly offbeat 'kittenish' would be better than both.

A simple activity that might support the idea of the right word in the right place would be to gather words that children know and use frequently, and so are in a position to exercise judgement. Greeting words or phrases to communicate 'hello' or 'goodbye', for example, would be suitably familiar. These can be collected over a week and then compared for different levels of formality, use by different age groups, regional variations, uses that come in and out of fashion, different modes such as written, spoken or text-speak, or why children might select a different form, depending on who they are speaking to. Selecting characters from books, and deciding which form they are likely to use, might create an opportunity to explore the subtleties of word choice as well as the subtleties of character. In this context, the best choice might be something as simple as 'see ya' or as eccentric as 'TTFN', or as archaic as 'Farewell'.

Teaching activities

The right word in the right place: Generating vocabulary to complete a diamante poem

Learning objective: To understand how even slight variations in word choice can shift meaning

Here is a diamante poem generated by creating a word bank of words prompted by the initial word 'monsters':

Monsters

Creepy, sinister

Hiding, lurking, stalking

Vampires, werewolves, mummies and zombies

Chasing, pouncing, eating

Hungry, scary

Creatures

The children were given the following pattern as the shape for the poem

Noun 1

Adjective adjective

Verb+ing verb+ing verb+ing

noun noun noun noun

Verb+ing verb+ing verb+ing

Adjective adjective

Noun 2

The aim would be to generate many more words than are required and then to make choices about the effect, the order, the sound or the rhythm of words. Talk should focus on explanation for word choice or why one word might precede another. The poem might become increasingly scary and so the words might intensify. This idea of heightening a mood through word choice might apply just as well to a narrative where some words might be held back purposefully to allow for an atmosphere to build.

An alternative activity would be to suggest starting and ending nouns that are antonyms, in which case the movement from one word to the next would need to shift meaning through the poem.

Day

Bright, sunny

Laughing, playing, doing

Up in the east, down in the west

Talking, resting, sleeping

Quiet, dark

Night

This poem has not followed the previous pattern and has, instead, created an antonym as the middle line of the poem, contrasting 'up and down' and 'east and west'. Requiring a contrast of opposites, an antonym, in the pattern, might allow for a discussion of the value of contrasting pairs in writing.

Synonyms can also be important for cohesion and to avoid repetition. Consider this example from *Outside Your Window: A First Book of Nature*, by Nicola Davies, which demonstrates how many different ways she has found to refer to dandelions.

Dandelions bloom like little suns. But **the flowers** don't last long — **they** fold up **like furled umbrellas** pointing at the sky. Then **each rolled umbrella** opens into a **puff of down: a hundred fluffy parachutes**, each carrying a small brown seed. Just one blow and you can set **them** flying.

Examples such as this might be useful to support a focused revision task, when children review their own writing for repetition; developing different ways of referring to the same thing. In this example, the differences include using a generic noun (flower) and a specific noun (dandelion), a pronoun (they) and several different noun phrases using different premodifying adjectives.

The aim of all these activities is not only to raise awareness of the wealth of possible synonyms but also to develop and practise authorial control, by encouraging children to explain why they choose one word over another.

Words can take different forms

Focusing on synonyms and antonyms can help to build a richer vocabulary; however, considering how the same word can take different forms can also present alternatives for young writers. Focusing on families of words can raise awareness of alternatives. The prevailing tendency to teach adjectives as a tool for adding description has already been noted in this book, as has the fact that there are other ways to add descriptive detail. A simple strategy is to point out that many adjectives might also take the form of an abstract noun or an adverb — for example, *dark, darkness, darkly*. Being aware of this variety is only halfway to reflecting on choices; the next step is to consider how this might impact on a possible sentence. 'A dark castle in the forest', therefore, might be re-formed as 'a castle whose darkness struck fear' or as 'a castle sitting darkly in the forest'. You can ask children to volunteer examples from their own work that use an adjective to premodify a noun, and challenge other children to first suggest the abstract noun or the adverb, and then to try to construct a sentence that uses these different forms. Such changes might make an interactive display within the classroom that is frequently changed. The aim is to trigger similar choices in subsequent writing tasks.

Words ending in 'ing' are another group of words whose grammatical form can change with use. Consider the following three sentences. How would you classify 'hunting' in each case?

- The children enjoyed hunting for Easter eggs.
- Have you read 'The Hunting of the Snark' by Lewis Carroll?
- The bullet was in the pocket of the hunting jacket.

In the first sentence, *hunting* is a verb; in the second, a noun; and in the third, an adjective. A possible talk activity is to try to explain why this is so in each case. A problem-solving activity exploring this further would be to set a challenge to use 'ing' words as nouns, adjectives or verbs. The task might pose the following questions:
Can all of these words be used as a noun?
Can all of them be used as an adjective?
Can all of them be used as a verb?

hunting	running	stirring	finding
shining	following	sighing	borrowing

While this is not building vocabulary in the strictest sense, it does focus on the way the same word can function in different ways within the sentence.

This variability of form extends to the spelling of the words themselves, a feature of English that makes it especially difficult to master in written form. In English, words with the same spelling can be pronounced differently: 'they were having a row about which row to sit in'. Words with different spellings can be pronounced in the same way: 'the roe deer grazed under the row of trees'. Words with the same spelling and the same pronunciation can mean different things: 'row upon row of spectators enjoyed watching Steve Redgrave row for victory'. However frustrating this might be for teachers and learners alike, the peculiarities of English can also capture the imagination. As much as teachers try to generate rules and reveal patterns, children will often be more interested in the anomalies and exceptions. Challenging children to find the exceptions can be one way of exploiting or exciting a curiosity for words and language. A spelling challenge that might also develop vocabulary could be to explore words that end with -able or -ible. A rule of thumb is that, for words ending in 'able', the main part of the word (i.e. the bit that comes before the -able ending) is usually a complete word in itself — for example, *likeable*, *fashionable*. For words ending in 'ible', however, it is less likely that the part before the ending will be a known word — for example, *incredible*, *horrible*; there are no such words as 'incred' or 'horrib'. So the challenge might be to find examples that conform to the rule of thumb, and examples that don't. Perhaps an additional challenge might be to work out if there is any rule for what happens to words that end in 'e'; for example, *believable* loses the 'e' but *loveable* keeps it. The focus here is on building banks of words, spotting patterns and talking about the meanings of words that are unfamiliar. It would even be possible to create words using this pattern — for example, something that makes you smile might be 'smileable'.

Wordplay is something of a national pastime and takes many forms: puns, tongue-twisters, anagrams, riddles, spoonerisms and palindromes, for example, are all ways of playing with words that can have a place in the classroom. Children will not have to look far to spot that others take pleasure in this kind of wordplay too. In Exeter, we have a carpet shop apparently owned by Walter Wallcarpet; a quick browse of the internet looking for 'puns on vans' reveals a bouncy castle supplier called 'Mission Inflatable' and a van selling kebabs proclaiming the services of Jason Donervan. A good source of puns can be found in the work of Simon Drew, who combines his word jokes with visual images; you might like to check out 'poultry in motion' and 'joined up whiting'. Similarly, the American children's poet J. Patrick Lewis uses wordplay to explore what a hippopotamusn't do and what a hippopotomust!

While it might be unrealistic to expect children to generate puns themselves, this focus on wordplay can spark an interest in words, generate conversation about how these word jokes work, increase vocabulary and encourage a habit of noticing language in use.

Words are always changing

Noticing language in use acknowledges that language is a living system that is always changing. A simple piece of research you might initiate is to ask children to find three words or phrases their grandparents used that are not used now, three words or phrases their parents used that are not used now, and three current words or phrases they use that neither their grandparents nor their parents used when they were younger.

An example of this change is the way two words can become one through common usage. Football, for example, is a single word, while golf ball is two. The use of hyphens can often be a staging post for a word that is in the process of being thought of as a single unit. This is why advice can vary on the use of hyphens. Is it, for example, play group, play-group or playgroup? The emergence of compound nouns demonstrates a certain creativity in language use that is mirrored in the teaching activity below, which makes use of kennings. The kenning was used in Anglo-Saxon and Norse poetry to create fresh, new descriptions of well-known things. Here are some examples:

- banhus (bone house) for body
- hron rad (whale road) for sea
- helmberend (helmet carrier) for warrior.

The kenning is a way of creating new nouns. It always involves at least two words, usually two nouns.

So a kenning is a compound noun. We have lots of modern kennings, of a very practical variety, such as *beachcomber, lawnmower, dishwasher* and *toothbrush*.

Teaching activities

New words from old: Generating kennings to write a poem that captures an object in new words

Learning objectives: Understanding how compound nouns (kennings) can be used to create description

Explain what a kenning is. Share the following example by Tony Mitton and ask the children what they think it describes. (Just in case it isn't obvious — it is a feather!)

A bird-dresser

a wind-presser

a pillow-filler   .

a poet-quiller

an arrow aimer

a dust tamer

a cobweb-breaker

a tickle-maker

Provide several objects that might be described using kennings and invite children to choose an object. In pairs, children can generate kennings, sharing their ideas with the wider group. They can then work individually, selecting the kennings from the pool that has been created, considering how well each kenning represents the object, how they sound and how they should be positioned in relation to the other kennings. Encourage the children to hear the poem out loud and to try out different combinations.

Kennings are created by joining two nouns; another way that new words are created is by fusing them, taking some of one word and some of another. In my own home, the lumpy custard so evocative of school meals was called 'lumpstard'. This can also be done with verbs — for example, *guess* and *estimate*, making *guesstimate*, or *squirm* and *wiggle* making *squiggle*. In his poem 'Jabberwocky', Lewis Carroll creates 'chortled' from chuckle and snorted and 'galumph' from gallop and triumph. 'Jabberwocky' is perhaps the best-known example of word creation and, while the words do not exist, we all have a sense of what they mean.

'Twas brillig, and the slithy toves

Did gyre and gimble in the wabe:

All mimsy were the borogoves,

And the mome raths outgrabe.

A group of older primary children might be able to write dictionary definitions for the terms and compare their results. Alternatively, they might try inventing their own words. Here are some things they might try.

1.   Invent a verb for when you call someone on their mobile phone, letting it ring only once in order to save money.

     For example: 'I'll _____ you when I get home safely.'

2.   Invent a verb for that awkward moment when you can't introduce somebody because you can't remember their name.

     For example: 'It was so embarrassing. I completely _____ her.'

3.   Invent a verb for when you are expecting a visitor and you keep checking outside your door to see if they have arrived because you think you might have heard them.

     For example: 'I've _____ five times already.'

As it happens, other languages do have words for these situations:

* number 1 is 'prozvonit' in Czech (or 'dar un toque' in Spanish)
* number 2 is 'to tartle' in Scottish
* number 3 is 'iktsuarpok' in Inuit.

Finding opportunities to talk about the words and the language we use is key to building a broad vocabulary. Developing a habit of noticing language features, and encouraging curiosity about patterns and deviations from patterns is all part of how this building is facilitated. So whether this is attention to the subtle difference simple word changes can make, or the contrast of pairing words with opposite meanings, whether it is playing with form and structure, or whether it is generating new ways to say what you mean, it is well-chosen vocabulary that will bridge the gap between intention and realisation. It is worth giving time therefore to the simple pleasure of playing about with words.

8
Standard English

> **Grammar joke**
>
> Q: When does a dialect become a language?
> A: When its speakers get an army and a navy.

What you need to know

Standard English (SE) is one *variety* of English. It is a variety that isn't attached to a particular geographical region, although it is often associated with the south-east of England. Instead of a geographical connection, it is related to social class: it is strongly associated with high social status and power. In this sense, SE is a *prestige* variety of English: it is valued above other varieties, and people are often socially judged on their ability to use it.

The importance of teaching children to use SE is enshrined in the Teachers' Standards, where all teachers are required to 'promote' its use (DfE, 2011). However, defining SE is not always straightforward, particularly because it is constantly evolving, and because it can be found in formal *and* informal varieties. In this chapter, we will look at some of the distinguishing features of SE, attitudes towards it, and how you should approach teaching it. We will also look at the difference between non-standard English and informal or **colloquial** language, and the difference between SE and linguistic 'etiquette'. Teaching SE should be accompanied by an understanding that other varieties of English are also important: children need to feel that their identity and heritage — often embodied in local **dialects** — is valued, while still learning to use SE where appropriate.

What is Standard English?

Standard English is a variety of English that tends to be used by the most powerful members of society, and within the most powerful institutions and contexts. Some linguists call it a dialect, but it has no geographical association, so unlike most other dialects it doesn't provide any information about where the speaker comes from. It is widely understood but not widely produced: spoken English tends to be more non-standard, and SE is required in only some types of writing. David Crystal sums this up in his definition of SE as 'a minority variety (identified chiefly by its vocabulary, grammar and orthography) which carries most prestige and is most widely understood' (1995: 110).

SE can be spoken in any **accent** but is often associated with the accent known as **received pronunciation** (RP), the accent that carries most prestige. Thus, some people write and speak of 'BBC English' (meaning SE) and a 'BBC accent' (meaning RP), referring to the language used in formal broadcasts such as news programmes (though any time spent listening to or watching BBC output will usually reveal a range of accents).

Unlike the Académie Française, which acts as an official authority on the Standard French language, there is no official body that protects, defines or pronounces judgement on the rules of SE. Grammatical forms, words and spellings generally become standardised through widespread use and inclusion in various dictionaries and grammar books. Consequently, SE is an evolving entity. Grammatical constructions that were considered non-standard in the past become subsumed into SE over time. A current example of this is the **subjunctive** form of the verb 'to be': the once standard use of the subjunctive in sentences such as 'I wish I were on holiday' is now being widely replaced by the less formal but still arguably standard construction 'I wish I was on holiday' (more about the subjunctive later).

Why is Standard English important?

The association between SE and social prestige makes it an important 'educational target' (Crystal 1995: 110). If it is the linguistic variety of the powerful and of powerful institutions, then it follows that being able to use it is empowering, enabling the users to succeed within powerful institutions such as education, the government and the law courts.

There is also significant prejudice towards other varieties of English, despite the fact that regional dialects often have features that are more sophisticated than SE. A famous example of this is seen in a 1995 BBC interview on the *Today* programme with Norman Tebbit, then chairman of the Conservative Party:

> ... if you allow standards to slip to the stage where good English is no better than bad English, where people turn up filthy at school ... these things tend to cause people to have no standards at all, and once you lose your standards then there's no imperative to stay out of crime.

While this logical leap, which links poor 'standards' of English to a life of crime, may seem rather antiquated, a similar position was taken in an article published in the *Evening Standard* in 2011, in which the author linked the violent actions of the London riots to the 'wilful distortions' and 'tedious double negatives' of 'inchoate street slang' (Johns, 2011).

These misunderstandings of language variety (the fact that the street slang seemed 'inchoate' to Johns shows how adept the young people have been in inventing a slang that excludes listeners who aren't part of their social group) reflect another important fact: we are judged on our ability to use SE, both in speech and writing. While it is only a 'native' dialect to around 12–15 per cent of the population (Trudgill, 1999), children whose own dialect is SE or close to SE are advantaged by the fact that their dialect is considered to be socially preferable.

However, this does not mean that schools need to try to stamp out other dialects, or urge parents to stop speaking 'incorrectly' to their children at home. Dialects are important as they link us to a particular community, and they are therefore a significant part of our identity. Being able to enjoy and experiment with different ways of speaking can help children to understand how language works, and regional dialects can be assets in the classroom in much the way that an EAL child's home language can be a valuable resource: making the features of language more explicit by providing contrast. Children need to learn to be able to use SE when it is appropriate — both in speech and in writing. Moving between their home dialect and SE is called **code-switching**.

The grammar of Standard English

Despite the evolving nature of SE, there are some clear grammatical features that differ from many non-standard dialects. Crystal (1995) classifies these differences as grammatical (how words relate to one another to create meaning), lexical (to do with words) and orthographic (how words are written down).

We can look at a fictional non-Standard English variety to see some of these differences in action. Here is an analysis of the dialect spoken by Roald Dahl's BFG:

> The Giant let out a bellow of laughter. 'Just because I is a giant, you think I is a man-gobbling cannybull!' he shouted. 'You is about right! Giants is all cannybully and murderful! And they does gobble up human beans! We is in Giant Country now! Giants is everywhere around! Out there us has the famous Bone-crunching Giant! Bone-crunching Giant crunches up two wopsey whiffling human beans for supper every night! Noise is earbursting! Noise of crunching bones goes crackety-crack for miles around!'

Grammatical variation

Giant dialect	Standard English
The verb 'to be' has a regular form, which doesn't inflect for person: 'You is about right' 'I is a giant' 'We is in Giant Country' 'Giants is everywhere'	Irregular form: I am, you are, he is, we are, they are
Different form of 'to do' for third person plural present tense: 'they does'	they do

(Continued)

Grammatical variation (continued)

Giant dialect	Standard English
No distinction between subject and object plural pronoun: 'us has'	Distinguishes between subject and object plural pronoun: '<u>we</u> have'; 'it comes to <u>us</u>'
Different form of 'to have' for second person plural present tense: 'Us has'	we have
Absence of determiners before nouns that are not premodified: 'Bone-crunching' 'Noise is earbursting'	Determiners before common nouns, regardless of the presence or absence of premodification 'The Bone-crunching Giant' 'The noise is earbursting'

Lexical variation

Non-standard adjective formation, using different suffixes: cannibal — *cannybully*; murder — *murderful*	Adjectives are cannibal, murderous
Non-standard vocabulary: *whopsy, whiffling, (human) bean, earbursting* as a compound adjective, *crackety-crack*	Human being, ear-bursting

Orthographic variation

Cannybull (you could argue that this is lexical variation if you think this is a different word to cannibal)	Cannibal

You'll see from this that many of the grammatical non-standard features involve the use of pronouns and verbs and how they inflect. This relates to **subject–verb agreement:** the fact that the verb form changes according to the subject it is linked to, and particularly whether it is **first, second** or **third** person (I/we, you or he/she/they). The irregularity of the SE inflection of the verbs 'to be' and 'to have' is a particular contrast to many dialects, and some non-standard varieties don't show distinctions between **singular** and **plural** or first/second/third-person subjects, like the BFG's 'I is' 'You is' 'We is'.

Some key grammatical characteristics of SE are presented in the table below (adapted from Trudgill, 1999). You will see that, in many cases, SE is less sophisticated than the other varieties.

Standard English	Other varieties
Does not allow **double negatives**	Double negatives can often be used for emphasis, so 'I don't want none' is a stronger alternative to 'I don't want any'
Does not distinguish between second person singular and plural pronoun: 'you'	Often make singular/plural distinctions such as thou/you or you/youse

(Continued)

Standard English	Other varieties
Has two **demonstrative pronouns**: this (near the speaker) and that (away from the speaker)	Often have an extra demonstrative pronoun: this (near the speaker), that (near the listener) and yon (away from both)
Irregularly formed **reflexive pronouns**, e.g. 'myself' (based on possessive pronoun 'my'), 'himself' (based on object pronoun 'him' rather than 'his)	Often have regularly formed reflexive pronouns, e.g. myself, hisself
The verb 'to be' is irregular in present and past tense: am, is, are; was, were	Often has a regular form, e.g. I be, you be, he be; I were, you were

Formal and informal Standard English

It's important not to confuse SE with 'formal' language. While formal contexts for speech and writing usually *require* the use of SE, it can also be used informally. The following example comes from an article by Peter Trudgill (1999).

* Father was exceedingly fatigued subsequent to his extensive peregrination.
* Dad was very tired after his lengthy journey.
* The old man was bloody knackered after his long trip.

Trudgill explains that these variations are all examples of SE despite the fact that the first is very formal, and the last is very informal. The use of 'bloody knackered' highlights the difference between non-Standard English and colloquial language: colloquialisms that are widely understood regardless of your dialect background are *informal* but not necessarily non-standard.

In contrast, the following example (also Trudgill's) *is* non-standard, using a form of the verb 'to be' that is common to several regional dialects.

* Father were very tired after his lengthy journey.

Informal SE may, for example, use:

* widely understood colloquial words (e.g. kids, buzz off)
* contractions (e.g. can't, won't)
* abbreviations (e.g. phone instead of telephone)
* second or first person (e.g. 'You might' instead of 'One might').

Non-standard English will, by contrast, use:

* words that are recognisable only to people who understand a particular dialect (e.g. 'dimpsey' meaning 'twilight' in Devon; 'spelk' meaning 'splinter' in Newcastle; 'lass'; 'wee'; 'bairn'; 'blether'; etc.)
* grammatical constructions that differ to SE (e.g. 'the house what Jack built'; 'we was told').

Slang, by contrast, involves the use of language designed to be understood only by a particular social group (often adolescents), so while a colloquial version of 'very good' might be 'awesome', a dialect version might be 'proper job' (Devon), and a slang version might be 'bare dench' (originating from the London urban music scene).

The subjunctive

As mentioned above, the subjunctive is now relatively rare, but it is a form associated with very formal SE. It is used to express possibilities, opinions, intention — things that are not known to be facts. It's seen often in the form of the verb 'to be' in phrases such as 'If I were you', 'If we were to go . . .' (rather than 'If I was' 'If we went').

This form of the subjunctive is an interesting stem or pattern to use for imaginative poetry, as can be seen in action in A.A. Milne's 'If I Were King':

I often wish I were a King,

And then I could do anything.

If only I were King of Spain,

I'd take my hat off in the rain.

The subjunctive can also be used to convey the importance of something, and in this instance the verb used takes a simple form. The simple form is the infinitive minus 'to', so 'go' instead of 'to go' and 'be' instead of 'to be' in the examples below.

*   We recommend that he **go** to a specialist. (Compare 'goes to a specialist'.)
*   It's essential that they **be** able to recite a full list of the kings and queens of England. (Compare 'are able to'.)

You could consider using this more sophisticated pattern when teaching older children to write formal letters.

'Linguistic etiquette'

SE should not be confused with the 'rules' of linguistic etiquette, such as 'don't split an infinitive' or 'don't end a sentence with a preposition' (the latter famously embodied in the sentence often — probably incorrectly — attributed to Winston Churchill: 'This is the sort of English up with which I will not put'). These rather arbitrary 'rules' stem largely from the preferences of individual writers in the nineteenth and early twentieth centuries, such as Henry Alford, writer of *Plea for the Queen's English* in 1869, and there is no particular rationale behind them. An etiquette 'rule' that is more widespread today is that sentences shouldn't start with a co-ordinating conjunction such as 'but' or 'and'. It's worth noting that, while starting with a conjunction is *informal*, it is not *non-standard*. And many authors break this 'rule', particularly when writing speech. Here is an example from Diana Wynne Jones' *Howl's Moving Castle*:

> 'They're expecting it,' Howl said. 'You should only have to wait most of the morning. Tell them a child could work it. Show them. And when you come back, I'll have a spell of power for you to get to work on.'

Speech and writing differences

As mentioned earlier, SE is more common in written rather than spoken contexts. When SE is spoken, it tends to be more informal, using more colloquial words, phrases and contractions. We rarely speak in full sentences, and tend to favour **co-ordinated** chaining over **subordinate** embedding of **clauses**. We are also able to make use of non-verbal communication, so may use more **demonstrative pronouns** (there, that) that we can support with gesture, and can usually have immediate feedback from the listener, which means that ambiguity and incompleteness is often more acceptable than in writing, and that repetition, corrections and interruption are common.

Because of the link between SE and writing, non-standard varieties in print tend to be found in **direct speech** (the words a person or character is reported as saying), as in the extract from *The BFG* above. This provides an opportunity to help children to understand the features of SE by comparing it to other dialects. Another example you might like to use is taken from Janet and Allen Ahlberg's *Burglar Bill*:

> He creeps up to the box and raises the lid.
>
> 'Blow me down,' he says. 'It ain't no police cars, it's a . . .'
>
> '. . . baby!'
>
> Burglar Bill puts the baby on the table.
>
> 'What was you doing in that box, baby?' he says.
>
> But the baby only keeps on crying.
>
> 'All alone,' says Burglar Bill. He pats the baby's little hand. 'A orphan!'
>
> But the baby only keeps on crying.
>
> Then Burglar Bill says, 'I know what you want — grub!'

Have a go at identifying the non-standard features in Burglar Bill's speech (answers at the end of the chapter).

Reading books like this creates an opportunity for discussing how we all talk differently. It also shows how making a character speak in dialect is a good way to help us to imagine them: it helps us to 'hear' how they speak and gives us information about their background — where they come from and their social status.

Speech marks

The appearance of dialogue in examples like *Burglar Bill* provides an opportunity to teach children about speech marks. These are inverted commas, which can be single (' ') or double (" "), used to mark out direct speech. Inverted commas may also be used as **quotation marks** to mark out a section of text that has been quoted from elsewhere, or as **scare quotes** to draw attention to ironic or unusual use of a word or phrase, or to highlight a word or phrase that is being discussed, e.g. we call this punctuation 'inverted commas'.

Teaching Standard and non-Standard Englishes

Looking back at educational policy, *The Bullock Report* (DES, 1975) offers useful advice about how to approach the teaching of SE:

> It seems to us far more reasonable to think in terms of appropriateness rather than absolute correctness . . . the aim is not to alienate the child from a form of language with which he has grown up and which serves him efficiently in the speech community of his neighbourhood. It is to enlarge his repertoire so that he can use language effectively in other speech situations and use standard forms when needed.

We therefore suggest the following principles.

- Focus on understanding language and knowledge about language, rather than 'correctness'.
- Talk about both Standard and non-Standard English.
- Encourage language investigation, especially of local dialects.
- Remember that language variation is not just regional, but social too.
- Support children in becoming confident code-switchers, able to use SE with ease where appropriate.

Teaching activities

Language Detectives: Exploring English varieties

Learning objective: Understand some ways in which a local dialect differs from SE.

Start with a short list of local dialect words. Ask children if they know what they mean, and write down any other dialect words that they know. Ask them what is special about these words.

Play a clip of someone speaking in the local dialect, then someone speaking in SE (e.g. from www.bbc.co.uk/voices). Discuss with children the differences between the two, drawing out a few specific examples of comparisons. Ask them what you would call these different ways of speaking. Explain or elicit the difference between dialect and accent, then define the following.

- **Dialect:** a version of English that is used by a particular group of people, e.g. (write examples from the local dialect and explain where it is spoken).
- **Accent:** the way that words are pronounced by a particular group of people.
- **Standard English:** the version of English that is understood by most people across the country, used in writing and sometimes in speech.

Then, either with extracts printed out or audio versions already prepared, or allowing children to use www.bbc.co.uk/voices, ask them to be 'language detectives' and find out as much as they can about their local dialect. You could prepare resources to help them to write down 'dialect words' or 'dialect phrases', and give them a list of SE grammatical forms to look out for and compare with the dialect they read or listen to. For example:

Standard English	'xxx dialect'
Pronouns: I, me, my, myself You, your, yourself He, She, His, Her, Himself, Herself Them, their, themselves	
To be: I am, you are, he is, she is, they are I was, you were, he was, she was, they were	
To have: I have, you have, he has, she has, they have I had, you had, he had, she had, they had	
Isn't	

To scaffold this further, you could complete the second column with some features from the local dialect, and ask children to highlight or tick them off when they find them. This could lead in to homework where children investigate their local language further (e.g. interviewing local people who speak the dialect) or a piece of writing that uses dialect forms. It could also lead to a display about the local dialect, which could be added to over time as children find more examples of words and phrases.

Talk about it!

- The trick here is to avoid talking about 'incorrect', 'wrong' or 'proper' English, and to focus the talk on what is 'standard' versus what is the local 'dialect'.

- To begin with, try asking open questions about the dialect words and examples to see how the children think about language — for example, 'What do you notice about these words?', 'What is special about these words?', 'What is different about these words to how we normally speak in school?', 'What is different about these two ways of talking?'

- Once you've explained the terms 'dialect', 'accent' and 'Standard English', try to reinforce understanding by using them as often as possible so, rather than saying 'that's wrong' about a grammatical form, say 'that's not Standard English' or 'that's a dialect phrase'.

- You also need to be very careful not to conflate SE with 'posh' or 'formal' language. Talking about SE as the language 'that everyone can understand, not just people who live here' can be a way around this.

Notes for teachers

1. EAL children will need careful consideration here, but, depending on their level of English, it may be particularly helpful for them to begin to understand that there is a difference between SE and the language that they might hear people speaking locally.

2. Your own children may have widely different experiences and understandings of the local dialect. This can be an opportunity for some children to become 'experts'.

3. Consider inviting in a local dialect speaker to bring this to 'life' — you are likely to be able to find fun online resources.

4. Looking for dialect words will be the most straightforward activity, but try to support children in finding some of the grammatical differences too — the table above, with pronouns and verb forms, aims to do this.

Creating characters: Adventures in Pirate English

Learning objective: Understand how to create a character's voice through the use of non-standard English

---

Display the following extracts from *The Pirate Cruncher* by Jonny Duddle:

I'll show ye my map if ye'll take me there.	Ye cannot imagine the booty that's there!	I'd like to fill me boots with lots of Loot!

Ask children to read these sentences aloud. If any do 'pirate' accents, ask them why they're doing that (if not, ask them what sort of people they think might say these sentences). Draw out the ideas that relate to pirates (maps, treasure). Show them that it's not only *what* is said that makes us think of pirates, but also *how* it is said.

Then ask them how a teacher, rather than a pirate, would say these sentences. Tell them that they may have to change one or two words. Model: 'I'll show you my map if you'll take me there.'

Highlight the words that have changed (all personal pronouns: 'ye' to 'you' and 'me' to 'my'). They may want to change 'booty' and 'loot' to 'treasure' too. Tell them that they've changed the pirate version of English into *Standard English*.

Show the following further phrase from *The Pirate Cruncher* and ask them to change this into SE too:

> That sounds just like our sort of plunder or my name ain't Pirate Purplebeard of Penzance.

Discuss the effect of 'ain't' in this sentence. How does it help us to imagine Pirate Purplebeard? What does it make us think about him?

Read *The Pirate Cruncher* (or another suitable pirate-themed book) with children, enjoying and discussing the story together. Then, using the following phrases on cards, ask them to sort them into two groups: 'Pirate English' and 'Standard English'.

To the ship me lads!	To the ship, my boys!
Ahoy! What be ye seeking?	Hello! What are you looking for?
There ain't nothing like Pirate gold!	There isn't anything like Pirate gold.
Aye lad, there be treasure in them hills.	Yes boy, there is treasure in those hills.
Yon ship be the finest in t' seven seas.	That ship is the finest in the seven seas.
Avast! Yon lurks t'Kraken	Look out! The Kraken lurks over there.

Compare answers and together create a crib sheet of how to speak Pirate English. For example:

Instead of . . .	Use . . .
I am, you are, she/he is, this is	I be, you be, she/he be, this be
Isn't, Is not	Ain't
You	Ye
My	Me
Those	Them
That	Yon
The	T'
Look out	Avast
Hello	Ahoy

Ask children to invent their own pirate character, and write a few sentences in Pirate English for them to say. Share their ideas and discuss the effect of writing the pirate speech in Pirate English instead of SE — it helps to create a sense of the pirate's character, it helps you to imagine how they're speaking.

Older or more able children can then develop this into a pirate story, where narrative is written in SE and the speech in Pirate English, or do a slightly easier activity where they write a short play script or conversation to act out entirely in Pirate English.

Talk about it!

- In the starter activity, try to explore the children's implicit knowledge of pirate dialect through open questions such as 'Who might talk like this?', 'What makes this sound like a pirate?' You may also need to talk about the distinction between accent and dialect here: when you read it out, you're saying the words in a pirate accent — what is it about *the way that it's written down* that makes you do that?

- You will then need to use talk to draw out the impact of writing direct speech in a particular dialect. Open questions to use here might go along the lines of: 'How does it help us to imagine the character?', 'What does it make us picture?', 'How does it help us to imagine or hear what they sound like?', 'What does it tell us about them?'

- Again, be careful to avoid talking about SE as 'proper', 'correct' or 'formal'. The contrast between Pirate English and 'How would a teacher say this?' is intended to be a way around this — highlighting that different varieties are spoken by different people rather than that one is 'right' and one is 'wrong'.

Notes for teachers

1. This lesson does assume familiarity with 'pirates' and is not sensitive to children who are immigrants, who may have had encounters with modern piracy, so please consider carefully whether it is appropriate for your children, and adapt to a different dialect if necessary (e.g. using Burglar Bill and 'cockney' dialect instead).

2. You will find several pirate-name generators online that you could use with children (check first that they are appropriate for children!), and you could link this activity to International Talk Like A Pirate Day (see www.talklikeapirate.com). You might also find some pirate shanties to play.

Games box

I was walking: Children sit in a circle. The first starts a short story like this: 'I was walking down the road when I saw . . . [e.g. a pink dog]'. The second then says to the first, 'You were walking down the road when you saw a pink dog', then adds their own 'I was walking down the road when I saw a giant spider crushing a lamppost'. The third student then says to the second, 'She/he was walking down the road when . . . You were walking down the road when. . .', then adds their own 'I was walking down the road when I saw. . .'. This continues round the circle. You can adapt this, e.g. 'I was sailing on the sea'; increase/decrease the number of turns that children have to remember; adapt it to present tense. As well as being a memory game, it reinforces standard verb inflections of 'to be', and you could also adapt it for the verb 'to have': 'She has a purple ladybird. You have a tapdancing bumblebee. I have a turtle called Horatio'.

Could've — should've — would've: Tell (or elicit) the tale of Little Red Riding Hood. Together, write advice about what she *should have* done, e.g. 'You should have listened to your mother'. Then write advice about what she *could have* done, then about what you *would have* done. Ask children to choose their favourite piece of advice and circulate around the room to say it as dramatically as possible to as many different children as they can. Demonstrate that they need to say *'ve* or *have* rather than *of*. This could lead into some drama activities around the fairy tale, and you could also adapt it for use with a different story.

Interpreter: Role-play an interview with a pirate and his 'interpreter'. One student is the pirate and speaks in Pirate English (see earlier lesson idea) and the other student acts as a translator, repeating what they say in SE.

Tell the teacher: Drop in some non-standard constructions when you're explaining a simple task and ask children to buzz/call out a particular word/put their hands on their head when they notice — then ask them to tell you how to say it in SE.

Tackling misconceptions

Differences in verb use between dialects and SE are the cause of some of the most common errors when writing SE. Errors will depend on your children and their linguistic backgrounds, but these are some common issues to look out for and explicitly teach:

The past tense of 'be', which in SE is conjugated differently than in regional dialects. For example:	
Cockney: You was great	SE: You were great
Devon: He were late	SE: He was late

Using the inflected past tense when the past participle is required. For example:	
He had went	SE: He went (went = inflected past tense; gone = past participle)
She was sat down	SE: She was sitting down (sat = inflected past tense; sitting = present participle)

Using the preposition of rather than the contracted verb 've. For example:	
I could of	SE: I could've
She should of	SE: She should've

Children will also tend to conflate accent with dialect (particularly because regional accents and regional dialects are closely linked). Try to keep reinforcing that dialects are the words that we say, and accents are how they sound when speak them. As mentioned above, they will also tend to link SE to 'formal' or 'posh' language. This link is easy to make, particularly because SE is the variety of the socially elite, and generally has to be used in formal contexts. Try to reinforce the fact that it can be informal too, and focus explanations on the fact that it's the language that is understood by people across the country rather than being linked to a particular place.

Answers

Non-standard features are in bold.

He creeps up to the box and raises the lid.

'Blow me down,' he says. 'It **ain't no** police cars, it's a . . .'

'. . . baby!'

Burglar Bill puts the baby on the table.

'What **was** you doing in that box, baby?' he says.

But the baby only keeps on crying.

'All alone,' says Burglar Bill. He pats the baby's little hand. '**A** orphan!'

But the baby only keeps on crying.

Then Burglar Bill says, 'I know what you want — **grub**!'*

---

* Whether 'grub' is cockney dialect or now so commonly understood that you could consider it colloquial SE is debatable!

9

The role of talk

Grammar joke

Don't you know the Queen's English?

Why, yes, I'd heard she was.

The value of talk for learning

Spending any time in a primary classroom will confirm the priority placed on talk as a strategy for learning. Few teachers can be unaware of the seminal influence of Vygotsky in informing a pedagogy grounded in the assumption that children's thinking is mediated through language, and that it is through language that children construct their knowledge and understanding of the world. As Corden puts it, 'thought is not merely expressed in words — it comes into existence through words' (2000: 7). Through talk, our ideas take shape and are shared with others, and through talk we modify our thinking in response to the ideas of others. Vygotsky represents the relationship between the teacher and the learner as one where a novice is supported by an expert, until the learner becomes independent; and talk is the medium through which this process is enacted. In primary classrooms neither teacher talk nor child talk is viewed as being primarily for the purpose of transmitting knowledge, but as an active and ongoing process of co-constructing understanding. From this perspective it is not so much 'what is said' that is significant for learning but 'that it is said'. Talk, therefore, is conceived not simply as a product of learning but an important process in supporting learning.

The work of Mercer and Alexander has been influential in signalling that a key role of the teacher is to manage talk activities to ensure that talk has particular qualities that can lift classroom talk to become genuinely exploratory (questioning and speculative) or dialogic (responsive to others and generating new possibilities). This then represents the ideal; however, in practice, research has revealed that classroom practice can become dominated by sterile question-and-answer patterns in which teacher talk predominates, single-word answers are the norm and that, far from offering opportunities for speculation and dialogue, interaction is limited to notionally right and wrong answers with only particular children taking an active part (Hargreaves, Hislam & English, 2002; Myhill, Jones & Hopper, 2005).

This pattern may well be a consequence of the practical realities of the classroom where interaction may be strongly driven by curriculum goals and not necessarily indicative of teacher competence or personal beliefs and value. It is worth reinforcing therefore the characteristics of teacher talk that Mercer (2000) identifies as typical of a lively talking and learning classroom. These include:

- using talk to guide understanding, and encourage reasoning and reflection, rather than to simply test knowledge
- different forms of questions or talk activities that prompt different kinds of thinking
- making links between current talk and prior learning and experiences
- encouraging wider participation.

In our own research, working alongside teachers to develop manageable talk strategies for primary classrooms, we highlighted a simple positive change whereby teachers consciously tried to change the most common interaction pattern: teacher–child–teacher–child by the pattern teacher–child–child–child–teacher. A necessary requirement of this pattern is that the original prompt has to be open enough to generate a variety of different possible answers, and children and teachers need to listen to one another, in order to build on what the previous speaker has said. Planning some talk prompts or questions in advance can help create focused talk that is well matched to the learning intention and likely to generate variety in talk activities.

Managing talk about language

In light of what is known about the value of talk for learning, one of the key principles informing our grammar pedagogy has been a strong focus on the use of talk. It is worth pointing out, however, that there are marked differences in speech patterns and writing patterns. Perera suggests that young children are fairly adept at hearing this difference and quickly develop an awareness that 'writing is not simply the language of speech written down' (1987: 17). Nevertheless, as young writers develop, it is in the shift towards a wider repertoire of more 'writerly forms' that the difference between able and struggling writers is especially marked. In part this is a consequence of the relationship between reading and writing, such that avid readers encounter and internalise a wider range of linguistic possibilities. In addition, however, there is an advantage conferred by middle-class patterns of speech that more closely resemble written forms. Talk about language choices makes explicit for many children what is unconsciously absorbed by a few. Talk about writing choices is therefore a fundamental principle of the pedagogy advocated in this book. This managing of classroom talk about language takes a variety of different forms, which you will have already noted in the teaching activities outlined:

- drawing attention to the grammatical choices made by authors in 'real' books
- discussing other grammatical choices that might have been made
- being explicit about how the grammatical choice of the author has shaped the meaning and the effect of the text
- discussing the grammatical choices they, as developing writers, have when they write
- hearing and evaluating these choices out loud

- explaining the grammatical choices they make as writers, and being explicit about how these choices shape meaning and the effect of their own texts
- developing a grammatical language to talk about choices
- being playful with language, by using talk to push language to its limits to develop linguistic awareness and experience.

Talk about writing choices can happen in preparation for writing, during writing and after writing. Teachers are perhaps familiar with preparing children for a writing task and with a plenary activity that might evaluate what has been written. It is perhaps worth drawing attention to how teachers might challenge children as they write to vocalise their choices and, more importantly, to explain what they are trying to achieve through this choice. Indeed the habit of 'thinking aloud' as part of the writing process, thereby hearing a suggested phrasing or word choice, might be shared and promoted as an individual strategy for young writers.

Learning from classroom interaction

One of the privileges of working with teachers in generating our research and teaching materials has been to observe classroom teachers managing talk activities that focus on the grammatical choices young writers make. It will not surprise you to discover that the teachers who shared their classrooms with us did not always get it right! Which of us does? Of course there were also those magical moments when new understanding, both that of teachers and children, was visible. In sharing examples from the classroom here, the aim is not to suggest there are good and bad teachers who make wise or ill-judged decisions. The aim is to acknowledge that any one of these examples could have happened in our own classrooms, and that by noticing what happens in talk episodes we might all develop our skills in managing talk effectively.

It does not always go right!

The first set of examples considers what goes wrong; this can be in relation to talk activities more generally or in relation to language in particular. In common with many studies into classroom interaction, our classroom observations included talk episodes where there was just too much teacher talk and children's contributions were monosyllabic or formulaic. Perhaps the most common examples in relation to language were the frequency with which children were asked to provide definitions, for example:

'What is a verb' — 'a verb is a doing word'

'What is an adjective' — 'an adjective is a describing word'.

While these answers might be comforting for teachers, they can mask a lack of understanding, and are not necessarily all that helpful in identifying verbs or adjectives. Contrast those examples with these:

Teacher: Give me nouns that describe the dragon, not adjectives.

Various children: jaws, wings, feet, armour, venom, strength.

The context for this question is a lesson focusing on how well-chosen nouns might be as useful for description as adding adjectives. The question is demanding because children need to understand what nouns and adjectives are in order to offer suggestions, and so the thinking required to respond to this prompt is rather different to offering a well-rehearsed definition. In this example the children obligingly offer nouns, but it is possible to imagine that some children might offer adjectives. A talk opportunity to discuss the relationship between nouns and adjectives might follow. Simply recording their suggestions using your own knowledge to put them into two lists will allow for such a comparison.

In this example an abstract noun, 'strength', is suggested and so, depending on the age and experience of the children, a conversation about the difference between an adjective, 'strong', and an abstract noun, 'strength', might be appropriate. In all of this, the key purpose of the task is to describe the dragon and so the skill of the teacher is to open up fruitful conversations about the choices available, while not letting the grammar overwhelm the original purpose. The talk should always return to how these choices shape meaning or create an effect, and should not focus on grammar per se.

In addition to the dominance of teacher talk and overly formulaic questioning, another typical observation of classroom interaction is spotting a missed opportunity. This might be a consequence of a teacher so focused on communicating a learning objective that an opportunity for learning is missed, or a teacher reluctant to push for an explanation of the precise nature of the grammar–writing relationship. Consider the following example. The teacher has invited children to comment on things they liked about their own writing and in this example it is a description of a killer whale:

Child: *Its tail was a deadly killer*

Teacher: So what was he using there — *its tail was a deadly killer?*

Child: A metaphor.

Teacher: Brilliant!

Here the teacher's talk suggests that the learning purpose of the episode is correctly identifying metaphors — there is no discussion of the appropriateness of the metaphor or what it might be evoking in its description. Potentially, a further missed opportunity lies in not pursuing whether the simple clause structure is a good choice or whether a noun phrase created from the clause might have offered different sentence possibilities (e.g. *Its tail, a deadly killer, thrashed on the water*).

The use of praise, as the teacher does here with 'Brilliant!' can be an effective motivator, but in order to maximise the potential of talk in the classroom, there also needs to be a climate in which exploring alternatives and challenging choices is both normal and safe. Contrast that example with this one, a similar discussion focusing on choices:

Child: First it was *dark brown eyes*, and I changed it to *penetrating eyes the colour of chocolate.*

Teacher: Most of us would think of chocolate as nice and smooth and something we would want, maybe not as penetrating.

Here the teacher is gently challenging the choice the child has made, inviting the writer to justify whether the choice of chocolate as an image created the appropriate connotations. In this single response, the teacher uses talk as a way of opening up thinking about the link between choice and the effect of that choice.

A third area where talk in the classroom can go astray relates to subject knowledge and this is often linked to a focus on labelling: it isn't only children who get in a tangle with grammar! One of the purposes of this book is to give you control over your own subject knowledge so you can make informed decisions about how to integrate it into your own teaching. Consider this example of a teacher getting confused about adjectives and abstract nouns:

Teacher: Who could spot me an adjective in there?

Child: Darkness.

Teacher: Darkness — yes so it's describing the state of the room.

Both the teacher and the child are happy that *darkness* is an adjective; it is after all a describing word. What confident subject knowledge can offer us, however, is not so much the ability to point out error, but the possibility of pointing out choice. There is a family of words here: *dark, darkness* and *darkly* — an adjective, an abstract noun and an adverb — and each offers the opportunity to describe the room. Knowing this means you can create a talk opportunity about this choice.

Here is one final example of teachers and children getting in a tangle about grammar. Armed with what you have learned in this book, what do you think about this talk episode, and what might you suggest regarding what matters in conversations of this kind?

Teacher: Who's got an example? The rest of you are going to tell me whether it's a noun phrase or not.

Child: *Big cornflakey eyes*

Teacher: So *eyes like big cornflakes*, is there a noun in there? What's the noun?

Child: Is it *cornflakes?*

Teacher: What's the noun? Can you tell me what a noun is?

Child: A thing . . .

Child: Is it a describing word

Teacher: Is a noun a describing word?

Child: It describes an object.

Magic moments

Although this section has been titled 'Magic moments', it is possible that you may be underwhelmed by the examples. There is little point in sharing remarkable and unusual moments that are unlikely to be replicated or are impossible to incorporate into your practice. These examples are quite ordinary moments of magic, moments that might be re-created in any classroom. The skills they require are an understanding of how to manage talk, and enough subject knowledge to create or to spot an opportunity for learning. They stand as examples of good practice in talking about grammar and writing, which we hope you will build on in your own practice.

The first pair of examples highlight the importance of setting up group or pair talk carefully so that the talk is focused and purposeful. Here both teachers initiate episodes of thoughtful discussion, because they initiated the talk carefully, explaining the purpose of the talk, and offering discussion prompts. The first is from a lesson looking at how a sense of place can be established through the use of noun phrases; the second is contrasting the effect on the reader when, at a key moment in the plot, the author reverses the subject and the verb in a sentence:

> Teacher: First of all we're going to focus on the crypt. I'm going to give you one minute to discuss the different ways the crypt has been described and I want you to tell me what impact, what effect this had on you as reader?

> Teacher: But he didn't write it like that . . . think about these questions: Why do you think he changed it around? Why have we got the verb first? What effect does it have on the reader? Talk about this in pairs.

It is remarkably easy to set up talk activities with a focus that is too vague, or where the teacher has done so much talking already there is little left to say, or where there are too many prompts and too much to talk about. In contrast, the examples above, with only a few well-chosen words of instruction from the teacher, initiated focused, meaningful peer talk, which then led to an effective whole-class feedback. It may be helpful to plan before the lesson how you will set up this kind of group talk, and a sequence of such talk episodes might build understanding very effectively across a lesson. It is worth pointing out that these examples consider both choice and the effect of that choice as a focus for discussion.

The second pair of examples are in the context of an ongoing classroom conversation, and they illustrate two teachers not ending an interaction sequence when a superficially 'correct' answer is received. Instead, in both instances, the teacher goes back to the child and invites him or her to explain or justify their answers further:

> Child: I can use appropriate words.

> Teacher: Tell me what you mean by 'appropriate' words?

> Child: Olden-day words.

> Teacher: Any examples?

***

> Teacher: Why do you think the writer has chosen to do that?

> Child: To make it more impactful.

> Teacher: What impact though? What impact do they want?

Both of these examples stand in contrast to moments where generalities are accepted and not developed. Examples of this might be:

- Why did you choose that as a good example? — because it is very descriptive
- I have added adjectives for effect

- I wanted to make my reader read on
- That word is more interesting.

A well-managed talk activity can create moments in a lesson when the relationship between a grammar choice and its effect are made explicit. Below are examples of the kind of responses that are possible; they all come from lessons we observed and reveal primary children making remarkably sophisticated observations.

- If you put a noun, you don't always have to use an adjective — if it's a good noun.
- Make people wait — put the noun at the end of the sentence.
- He calls it *a figure* . . . It's a good choice of noun because it's got that mystery about it.
- If you're trying to show a knight is brave, instead of saying he is brave, you could describe him, for example, say he has 'big muscular shoulders' and 'his face is like a map full of scars'.
- Asked about a non-finite verb a teacher had found in an example in their writing, 'snorting its fury', the child explained that it is effective to start with the verb because you get the sound first.

A talk activity

This activity is an example of how you can initiate talk that invites young writers to think creatively about grammar and language choices, and to be curious about how texts work. As an activity, it models how the talk might be set up and the discussion prompts you could use.

Using the opening section of *Secret Heart* by David Almond (see below), prepare cards with two lists of words printed on them: one list headed 'Nouns', with all the nouns in the passage, and the other headed 'Adjectives', with all the adjectives that appear in this passage. Hand out the cards to groups, and display the following prompts for their group discussion.

Talk prompts

These nouns and adjectives are taken from the opening paragraph of a children's story.

- Look at the nouns — what do you think this story will be about?
- Look at the adjectives — what do you think this story will be about?
- What kind of atmosphere might these nouns and adjectives create?
- There are more nouns than adjectives — why do you think this might be?

Share the reading of the full extract, and gather the children's initial responses to this, inviting them to explain how the opening makes them feel, what kind of story they think it might be, and whether it makes them want to read on.

Move back into groups to consider the language choices in this opening, giving the children the following talk prompts.

> The **tiger** padded through the **night**. **Joe Maloney** smelt it, the <u>hot</u>, <u>sour</u> **breath**, the **stench** of its **pelt**. The **odour** crept through the **streets**, through his open **window** and into his **dreams**. He felt the <u>animal</u> **wildness** on his **tongue**, in his **nostrils**. The **tiger** moved as if it knew him, as if it was drawn to him. **Joe** heard its **footpads** on the **stairs**. He heard its <u>long slow</u> **breath**, the <u>distant</u> **sighing** in its **lungs**, the **rattle** in its **throat**. It came inside. It filled the **bedroom**. The <u>huge</u> **head** hung over him. The <u>glittering</u> <u>cruel</u> **eyes** stared into him. The <u>hot</u> **tongue**, <u>harsh</u> as **sandpaper**, licked his **arm**. The **mouth** was <u>wide</u> <u>open</u>, the <u>curved</u> **teeth** were poised to close on him. He prepared to die. Then someone somewhere called:
>
> 'Tiger! Tiger! Tiger! Tiger!'
>
> And it was gone.

Talk prompts

In this opening, David Almond creates an image of a tiger, padding down the street and into Joe Maloney's bedroom.

- What is your impression of the tiger?
- How has David Almond created this impression through his choice of nouns and adjectives?
- Can you comment on the choice of nouns?
- Can you comment on the choice of adjectives?

There are no right answers to these questions, and children may interpret the language choices made by David Almond in different ways, so it is important to give these interpretations space. At the same time, part of the skill of managing effective talk about grammar lies in steering the conversation in such a way that there is room for unanticipated responses, but also that you ask questions that stretch children's thinking. Here you might draw out how physical and sensory this opening is, and how that is partly established through the choice of nouns that refer to parts of the body to create the physicality, and adjectives that evoke strong sensoriness (*hot, glittering, curved, harsh*). You might also draw out the prevalence of nouns over adjectives, and how descriptive many of the nouns are (*stench, odour, pelt, rattle, wildness*). This helps to dispel the view that descriptiveness can be achieved only through using lots of adjectives.

Like all of the activities in this book, this one focuses on creating contexts for talk that open up discussion of the relationship between grammar choices and meaning or effect. Sometimes, however, activities like this trigger a different kind of conversation that might be termed 'grammatical reasoning', where children begin to think more specifically about grammar itself. Below are comments made by a group of children in Year 6 in response to the question 'Are you surprised there are more nouns than adjectives?'

Child: I'm surprised because a noun is something you describe with an adjective and you can describe it with more than one adjective.

Child: Yes, there should be more adjectives.

Child: No, because you don't just describe things with adjectives.

Child: But because a noun is something you can describe with an adjective and you can use more than one adjective for a noun.

Child: But if it weren't for the nouns, there wouldn't be any adjectives.

Here we see the children using grammatical reasoning to play with ideas around what words can describe, with one child recognising that nouns, as well as adjectives, can be 'describing words'. They also reason together about the ratio of nouns to adjectives, with one child making the argument that you'd expect more adjectives than nouns because you can have more than one adjective with one noun, and another child making a counter-argument that you can't have an adjective without a noun.

Managing high-quality talk about grammar and language

We have been privileged to share many primary teachers' classrooms, and observe how they lead talk about grammar and language, and have been excited by the quality of what we have seen. Through these many observations, we have learned from them and have established some of the dos and don'ts of managing high-quality talk activities about grammar and writing. We have set these out in the table below.

Effective practice	Things to avoid
Do use the grammatical terms naturally as part of classroom discourse so that children hear them regularly	Don't focus on definitions and labelling as this can generate confusion and mask grammatical understanding
Do probe for *why* a choice has been made rather than what a choice is — invite children to explain, elaborate and justify choices	Don't accept every idea a child suggests Don't end question sequences too quickly when the child gives the answer you were looking for
Do take children's responses as the starting point for discussion, rather than the finishing point	Avoid spending too much time identifying and labelling grammar terms, rather than discussing the effect of grammatical choices
Do develop grammatical thinking rather than grammatical labelling	Don't give answers to grammar questions if you are not sure you are right!
Do model what you do when you don't know an answer to a grammar question	

This chapter has considered the importance of high-quality talk in helping children develop rich understanding of the relationship between grammatical choices and their effects in writing. We believe that the talk is crucial in allowing children to secure their own understanding, rather than simply learning to parrot the teacher's point of view, and in this way it is critical in promoting deep learning about language. A talking classroom is a learning classroom.

Endnote

Grammar joke

My English teacher told me: 'In English, a double negative forms a positive. In some languages, though, such as Russian, a double negative is still a negative. However, there is no language where a double positive can form a negative.'

I thought to myself: 'Yeah, right.'

This book has attempted to set out a clear explanation of the basic grammar required for teaching the primary (and secondary) curriculum, and is addressed to teachers, rather than students. We know from our own research, and from the research of others around the world, that teachers' subject knowledge of grammar is not always secure. We also know from our observations that weaker subject knowledge has a direct impact on what and how children learn about writing and language choices: the most vibrant and exciting writing classrooms were where teachers had confident subject knowledge of grammar. So if you know your subject knowledge is not as strong as you'd like it to be, use this book as a way to build your knowledge over time. Grammatical understanding is hard to cram: it needs to mature slowly like a good wine, over time. Dip in to this book regularly; use it to check when you are planning; and use it as a reference point when you are unsure.

At the same time, remember that this book focuses on grammar, and strategies for teaching writing drawing on grammatical choices. It is not a book on teaching writing. We would be worried if the teaching of writing became wholly focused on grammar! Our approach to grammar and writing is *part* of a pedagogy for writing, not the whole thing. A rich writing curriculum includes attention to many other important teaching strategies, including: establishing imaginative and engaging ways into writing; supporting children's use of the writing process — especially enabling revision; modelling and scaffolding writing; and providing relevant feedback and assessment. A rich writing curriculum also gives young writers some freedoms to choose what to write about, opportunities to write on digital platforms as well on paper, and the chance to write for real purposes and audiences. Finally, think about the value of bringing authors into your classrooms to work alongside your children, creating a real community of writers.

References

Bryson, B. (2009) *Mother Tongue: The Story of the English Language*. London: Penguin.

Corden, R. (2000) *Literacy and Learning through Talk*. Buckingham: Open University Press.

Crystal, D. (1995) *The Cambridge Encyclopaedia of the English Language*, 2nd edn. Cambridge: Cambridge University Press.

Crystal, D. (1996) *Discover Grammar*. London: Pearson Longman.

Crystal, D. (2004) *Rediscover Grammar*. London: Pearson Longman.

DES (1975) *The Bullock Report: A Language for Life*. London: HMSO.

DfE (2011) Teachers' Standards. Available at: https://www.gov.uk/government/publications/teachers-standards (accessed 20 March 2012).

Elley, W.B., Barham, I.H., Lamb, H. and Wyllie, M. (1975) The role of grammar in a secondary school curriculum. *New Zealand Council for Educational Studies* 10: 26–41.

Flood, A. (2015) National curriculum is damaging children's creative writing, say authors. Online at http://www.theguardian.com/books/2015/jun/23/national-curriculum-is-damaging-childrens-creative-writing-say-authors (accessed 24 July 2015).

Hargreaves, L., Hislam, J. and English, E. (2002) Pedagogical dilemmas in the NLS: primary teachers' perceptions, reflections and classroom behaviour. *Cambridge Journal of Education* 32(1): 2–26.

Johns, L. (2011) Ghetto grammar robs the young of a proper voice. *London Evening Standard*, 16 August. Online at http://www.standard.co.uk/news/ghetto-grammar-robs-the-young-of-a-proper-voice-6433284.html (accessed 16 August 2011).

Jones, S.M., Myhill, D.A. and Bailey, T.C. (2013). Grammar for writing? An investigation into the effect of contextualised grammar teaching on student writing. *Reading and Writing* 26(8): 1241–1263.

Mercer, N. (2000) *Words and Minds: How We Use Language to Think Together*. London: Routledge.

Myhill, D., Jones, S., Lines, H. and Watson, A. (2012) Re-thinking grammar: the impact of embedded grammar teaching on children's writing and children's metalinguistic understanding. *Research Papers in Education* 27(2): 139–166.

Myhill, D.A., Jones, S.M. and Hopper, R. (2005) *Talking, Listening, Learning*. London: Open University Press.

Perera, K. (1987) *Understanding Language*. Sheffield: NAAE.

Trudgill, P. (1999) Standard English: what it isn't. In Bex, T. and Watts, R.J. (eds) *Standard English: The Widening Debate*. London: Routledge: 117–128. Online at http://www.phon.ucl.ac.uk/home/dick/SEtrudgill.htm (accessed 5 April 2015).

INDEX

Adverb Group 36–49

Adverb
    modification 36–37
Adverbial 39–42
    adverbial clause 40–41
    adverbial mobility 42
    adverbial phrase 39–41
    non-finite clause 40–41
    noun phrase 40–41
    prepositional phrase 39, 41
    subordinate clause 40–41
Categories of adverb 37
    conjunct 38–39
    degree 37
    disjunct 39
    manner 37
    place 37
    reason 37
    time 37

Clauses 50–64

Clause
    co-ordinated clause 51–52 *see also* 71, 72, 75
    finite subordinate clause 53–54
    multiply-claused sentences 50 *see also* 66, 67, 71
    non-finite clause 55 *see also* 40–41
    relative clause 54–55
    restrictive and non-restrictive relative clause 55
    single clause sentences 51 *see also* 67, 68, 71
    subordinate clause 53–56 *see also* 40–41, 66, 71, 72, 75

Conjunction
    co-ordinating conjunction 51
    subordinating conjunction 53
Relative pronoun 54
Semi-colon 56–57

Creative Pedagogy for Teaching Grammar 1–9

Grammar
    contextualised 3 *see also* x
    descriptive 1
    in the National Curriculum 1, 2, 3
        see also xi
    prescriptive 1, 2, 9
Pedagogy
    authentic texts 6
    classroom discussion 5 *see also* 101–109
    classroom examples 4, 5, 6, 7, 8, 9
    creative imitation 7
    designing and crafting writing 7
    grammar and meaning 3, 5 *see also* 29
    grammatical terminology 4
    playfulness 8, 9
    summary of key teaching principles 3

High-quality talk, generating talk to
    develop understanding of how tense is used in diary writing 19–20
    develop understanding of verb order in a verb phrase 18–19
    draw out pupils' implicit knowledge of language varieties 98
    elicit grammatical reasoning 108–109

evaluate effects of choices 75

evaluate noun and adjective choice 107–108

explain choices 30–31

explore how co-ordinating junctions join single clause sentences 59

explore the differences between standard English and dialects 96

generate ideas 30–31, 33

help understanding that standard English is a particular variety of English 95–96, 98

model and explore how adverbial phrases create mood and atmosphere 44–45

orally rehearse phrasing 33

recognise that subordinate clauses can usually alter their position in a sentence 62

secure understanding of tense 19–20

understand how adverbials can add detail to imagery 47

understand sentence structure 75–76

understanding that subordinate clauses can provide additional detail 62

Misconceptions

a verb is a 'doing' word 20

actions expressed through words other than verbs 21

adverbs are -ly words 37–38, 48–49

comma used to mark sentence boundary 79

confusing dialect with accent 100

confusing standard English with 'formal' language 100

conjunct/conjunction confusion 49

co-ordinated sentences contain two joined simple sentences 63–64

differences between dialects and Standard English 99–100

difficulty identifying subject and verb 78

incorrect use of *however* as a conjunction 64

layering grammatical terminology 49

nested structures 34

noun phrase as incomplete 34

past tense of 'to be' 99

unhelpful acronyms 63

using inflected past tense in place of past participle 99

using preposition 'of' instead of contraction of the verb 'to have': '-ve' 99

word class mobility 34

Noun group 22–35

Adjectives 22, 27–29, 31–34
   Determiner 23–24, 27, 28, 31, 34

Noun
   abstract noun 24–25
   common noun 24
   concrete noun 24–25
   count noun 24–25
   non-count noun 24–25, 34
   proper noun 24, 29–32, 34

Noun phrase
   head noun 22, 23, 26, 34
   non-finite clause 27, 28, 32, 33, 34
      see also 40–41, 55
   post-modified 27–28, 30, 31
   pre-modified 27–28, 31–33
   prepositional phrase 27, 28, 31, 33, 34, 35
      see also 39, 41
   relative clause 27, 28, 31, 33, 34
      see also 54–55

Pronoun 25–26

Preposition 27

Suffix 23, 25

Punctuation

Brackets 58

Bullet points 73

Colon 56–58

Comma
   parenthetical commas 56
   to demarcate a subordinate clause 56
   to mark a sequence of co-ordinated clauses 56

Dash 58–59

Ellipsis 73

Exclamation mark 73

Full stop 73

Question mark 73

Semi-colon 56–57

Sentence 65–79

Clause elements 68
   adverbial 68, 72 *see also* 39–42
   complement 68
   object 68
   subject 68, 69, 70, 72
      see also 16, 55–56
   subject-verb inversion 69, 76
   verb 68, 69, 70 *see also* 10–21

Clause structure 71
  co-ordinated clause 71, 72, 75
  main clause 66 *see also* 50–51
  subordinate clause 66, 71, 72, 75
Sentences
  definitions of 65, 67
  structure of 68, 69
  variety of 69, 71
Sentence types 69
  command 70, 71, 76
  exclamation 70, 71
  major 69, 70
  minor 69, 70
  multi-clause 66, 67, 71
  question 70, 71
  single-clause 67, 71
  statement 68, 70, 71

Standard English 87–100
Accent 88, 95
  received pronunciation 88
Dialect 87, 89–91, 95
  demonstrative pronoun 91, 93
  double negative 90
  first/second/third person 90
  grammatical variation 89–90
  lexical variation 89–90
  orthographical variation 89–90
  reflexive pronoun 91
  subject-verb agreement 90
Language variety
  code-switching 89
  colloquial 87, 91
  formal 87, 91
  informal 87, 91
  slang 88–89, 92
Speech and Writing differences 93
  chaining clauses 93
  direct speech 93
  embedding clauses 93
Speech marks 94
  inverted commas 94
  quotation marks 94
  scare quotes 94
The Subjunctive 88, 92

Talk, The role of 101–109
Dialogic talk 101

Discussion (grammar for writing pedagogic
  principle) 102–103, 109
Exploratory talk 101
Speech patterns 102
Subject knowledge 104, 105

Teaching Activities
  adverbial phrases to add atmosphere
    and detail to description of a journey
    42–44
  adverbial similes to create vivid images
    45–47
  compound nouns (kennings) 85
  creating new words 85–86
  dialects used to convey character through
    direct speech 96–98
  differences between a local dialect and
    standard English 94–96
  grammatical patterns in commands 76
  joining co-ordinated clauses 59
  noun phrases to create a visual picture
    31–33
  order of modals, auxiliaries and lexical
    verbs in a verb phrase 18
  past and present tense in diaries 18
  simple noun phrases to imply character
    29–31
  subordinate clauses to provide additional
    detail in information texts 61
  synonyms to support revision 82
  varying sentence length and word order to
    heighten drama 74
  word choice and meaning 81–12
  word class mobility 82–83
  word families and spelling 83–83

Verb group 10–21
Aspect
  expressing future time 14
  past perfect 15–16
  past progressive 15–16
  present perfect 15–16
  present progressive 15–16
Inflection 13
Mood
  active 16
  passive 16
Syntax 11, 50

Tense
  past tense 13–14, 17, 19
  present tense 13–14, 19
Verb
  auxiliary verb 12, 17, 18
  base form of the verb 13
  command verb 11
  complex verb phrase 12, 15, 21
  finite verb 14–15, 26–27, 34
    see also 70
  infinitive 13, 15
  lexical verb 11, 18, 21
  modal verb 12, 15, 18
  non-finite verbs 14–15

  past participle 15, 17
  present participle 15
  simple verb phrase 12, 14, 21, 51
  verb phrase 12, 50, 51

Vocabulary 80–86

Antonym 82

Compound noun (Kennings) 84–85

Grammar and spelling 83–84

Hyphenated words 84

Pun 84

Synonym 80, 82

ESSENTIAL PRIMARY SCIENCE 2/e

Alan Cross and Adrian Bowden

2014
9780335263349 - Paperback

eBook also available

If you are teaching - or learning - to teach primary science, this is the toolkit to support you!

Highly respected and widely used, Essential Primary Science 2E blends essential subject knowledge with a vast array of teacher activities. Updated and revised throughout to reflect the requirements of the new National Curriculum, it covers the essential knowledge and understanding that you need; plus it offers over 200 great ideas for teaching primary science at KSI and KS2 - so no more late nights thinking up creative new ways to teach key concepts!

Written in a friendly and supportive style this new edition offers:

- Over 200 original and new activities to complement the new curriculum, ready for you to try out in the classroom
- Tips on how to ensure each lesson includes both practical and investigative elements
- Suggestions on how to make your lessons engaging, memorable and inclusive
- How to deal with learners' common scientific misconceptions in each topic
- Two new chapters on working scientifically and how to tackle assessment
- New up-to-date web links to quality free resources

Drawing on their own extensive teaching experience and understanding of the new National Curriculum, the authors provide the essential guide to teaching primary science for both trainee teachers and qualified teachers who are not science specialists.

www.openup.co.uk

 **OPEN UNIVERSITY PRESS**
McGraw - Hill Education